"The way you use your brain has everything to do with everything you do."

Brian Thwaits

 www.trafford.com

North America & International
toll-free: 1 888 232 4444 (USA & Canada)
phone: 250 383 6864 ♦ fax: 812 355 4082

Praise for Brian Thwaits
and his *Train Your Brain* presentations

"Brian Thwaits is an outstanding speaker. It is highly unusual to have a speaker who is able to keep an audience mesmerized!"
— *The Institute of Internal Auditors*

"Without exception, staff felt that it was the best professional development session they have ever attended."
— *Trillium Lakelands School Board*

"Brian enthralled the audience with his 'Train Your Brain' presentation. He struck the right balance between information and entertainment. He was the perfect keynote speaker to help us kick off the day."
— *General Motors of Canada*

"That was probably the best-received keynote address of our conference history. We've never had a session that was so entertaining!"
— *Alberta Services for Students*

"Not only did Brian's presentation set the mood for our event, but it also generated many passionate conversations. Our conference follow-up survey clearly shows that he was a hit."
— *Food Industry Credit Bureau*

"We have seen many motivational and educational presentations over the years, and Brian's counts as the most memorable among them."
— *Fairview College*

"Our staff raved about Brian's presentation. They found it entertaining, humorous, energetic and informative."
— *Ontario Ministry of Health & Long-Term Care*

"Every so often, you come across someone who is not only a skilled presenter but also has a passion for their topic. Brian Thwaits is such a person."
— *Mt. Diablo Unified School District*

"Our group was thoroughly captivated the entire time. Several said that it was the best session we've had at our annual meeting in recent memory." — *Janssen-Ortho Inc.*

"The consensus is that Brian Thwaits was the best received speaker in anyone's memory. People have been amazingly positive in their feedback. He was a hit!" — *Vanier College*

"Brian Thwaits definitely lived up to his reputation as an entertaining and informative speaker. Feedback from participants was impressive." — *Ontario Power Generation*

"From all of our feedback, there have been only positive comments. Brian's presentation was an overwhelming favourite." — *Halton Catholic District School Board*

"Brian's presentation was energizing, motivational and very entertaining. Our membership has not stopped talking about his presentation." — *Credit Institute of Canada*

"Brian's session was a great hit. Almost all assessments evaluated at a 5 on a 5-point scale!! He had people laughing and learning." — *Greater Edmonton Teachers' Convention*

"Brian Thwaits is both entertaining and educational. His ability to match wit with understanding is remarkable." — *Microsoft Canada*

"Brian's presentation was fabulous!" — *Humber College*

"Brian delighted, amazed and informed. His ability to transform scientific facts into cocktail party conversation starters is truly unbelievable. Who would have believed the brain is so stimulating?" — *Professional Administrators of Volunteer Resources - Ontario*

"Weeks later, staff are still talking about how much they enjoyed the afternoon and how much they gained from Brian's presentation." — *Toronto District School Board*

"Brian is an eloquent speaker. We found him to be thought-provoking and enthralling — and we highly recommend him." — *Ontario Treasury Board*

"The best keynote we've ever had!"   *– Hudson Valley College*

"In my many years of working in the industry, I have never seen such an overwhelmingly positive response to a particular speaker as in Brian's case."   *– Ontario Nursing Home Association*

"Thousands of students, parents and staff have listened to Brian over the years. His ability to keep the audience engaged, thinking and laughing is remarkable."   *– Niagara College*

"Honestly, I can't say I've ever seen anyone receive this kind of glowing feedback. On a scale of 1-5, Brian Thwaits generally received a 5+.   *– Human Resources Development Canada*

"Several called it the best Professional Development Day ever. Brian Thwaits has the ability to engage a diverse crowd and make people laugh, while also providing helpful information."   *– Saskatchewan Institute of Applied Science & Technology*

"Brian informed, educated and entertained. Feedback was 100% favourable. His skills as a presenter are superb."   *– York Region Small Business Enterprise Centre*

"Brian's fabulous opening keynote address was astute, entertaining and informative. We've never had a presentation that has been so well received by all in attendance."   *– Seneca College*

"Brian's enthusiasm is contagious, and his audience leaves the room refreshed and 'buzzing'. His message challenges each of us to think differently, to use our brains differently, and he provides practical suggestions for improving performance."   *– Industrial Accident Prevention Association*

"Brian Thwaits dazzled the crowd! The message was powerful and captivated the audience."   *– London District Catholic School Board*

"Wow! The presentation Brian delivered for us was fantastic. We've seen presentations on the brain before, yet never one quite like that. All in attendance spoke about it for months after."   *– Washington Mutual Bank*

THE BIG LEARN
smart ways to use your brain

BRIAN THWAITS

TRAFFORD

Contents

Author's Note

WARNING:

Do not read this book!

That is, don't *just* read it.

As will be more thoroughly explained in the following pages, reading on its own isn't really a very effective way to learn. And what would be the point of spending time with this book's content if you were to remember little of what you just read?

So, before you begin, please do yourself a big favour and get ready to truly comprehend and recall the material you'll be covering. Put down the book for a minute and gather a few learning supplies. A pen, a pencil, a highlighter, a notepad and a set of coloured markers would be a good start.

Feel free to use them liberally as you read and take notes, jot down your thoughts, underline, highlight and circle any of the text that is interesting or seems important to you.

Also, a blank page has been added at the end of each chapter. Please take advantage of this extra space to scribble any brain waves you may have while those ideas are still in your head.

By doing this, you'll become more actively involved in the learning process so that, when you're done, you'll have a much more complete understanding of the theories and concepts discussed in this book.

Foreword

The most undeveloped piece of property
with the greatest potential is between the ears.

Anonymous

Most of what we know today about how the human brain functions has been learned only recently. In just the past few years, the amount of brain research in the world has increased tremendously. The sheer number of neuroscientists now devoting their considerable time, energy and resources to the study of the inner workings of the brain is remarkable.

This ongoing research, along with the phenomenal technological advances in the field, have led to startling discoveries, turning conventional wisdom about how we use our heads practically upside down. It's time for us now to take this new-found knowledge and apply it to how we think, learn, read, write, solve problems, advertise products, market and deliver services.

To be honest with you, I have to admit that, as an educator, I've been as guilty as anyone of having perpetrated ineffective learning methods. As a corporate trainer, I've committed the same offenses. As a professional speaker, too, I know I've made mistakes.

For that, I'm sorry. I guess that, at the time, I just didn't know any better — because I used to think that everyone probably learned pretty well the same way: the way I learned when I was in school, the way I learned when trying to master a new job or a new skill.

As a student, I was pretty good at being successful by applying as minimum an effort as I could get away with, and I was actually kind of proud of myself for having what I figured were enough smarts to operate that way. After all, I was able to stay awake through lectures, take scant notes, and stay right out of most group discussions. Left to my own devices, I could usually cram information into my head well enough to not only pass tests, but even score well on them.

My 'system' was based mostly on the concept of rote learning taught in elementary school (paring down information into point-form notes, reading and rereading them, copying them out over and over, repeating the information aloud). It was both time-consuming and boring — but it seemed to work.

It was only natural, then, that I'd take this seemingly successful strategy into adulthood with me later on. So it came to pass that, at work, I'd listen to supervisors explain things to me (without asking questions, of course), browse through some manuals later on, make some mistakes when first attempting new assignments and, eventually, through trial and error, achieve a measure of competence. Good enough for me, I figured.

When I began my career as an educator, I applied those very same principles at the front of the classroom, believing that my students, too, should be capable of learning exactly the same way I did.

I figured that, if they took the time and made the effort, they'd do well. If they didn't, they wouldn't. I mean, it had worked for me, so it was bound to work just as well for them too, right?

Later on, as an instructor involved in the training of business managers, administrative support staff and industrial line-workers, I continued to use similar methods. Again, why wouldn't I?

And now the brain researchers come along and blow this theory right out of the water.

According to their findings, the way I studied and taught and trained was not only inefficient, it was actually an approach that made learning practically as difficult as it could possibly be.

What scientists began to discover many years ago, and have been reinforcing ever since, is the idea that most of us are using our brains in ways that are, in fact, almost opposite to the ways they actually work best. But we're all quite capable, they say, of learning better and faster by following simple principles that can harness the brain's enormous natural potential.

So why have we been learning so inefficiently for such a long time? How could it be possible that we've been so misled for all these years? Surely, the education system must have taught us how to learn properly! Ah, there's the rub. In fact, it seems that the school classroom might just have been, in many ways, the *origin* of many of our learning problems.

For instance, I remember when my teachers first started saying things like: "Read Chapter 4. We'll be having a test next week." Now, very often, that was all the information they gave us. There was no follow-up, no "... and now I'll show you exactly what to do so you'll achieve a decent mark on the test."

Just: "Read Chapter 4. We'll be having a test next week." Apparently, it was up to us to figure out the best way to handle this problem on our own, in spite of our youth and inexperience. So we went home with our books to prepare for this new challenge. And how did most of us do this? We read the chapter over a couple of times, that's how.

And, if this strategy got us a passing mark on that first test, we continued 'studying' this way for future tests. If, on the other hand, our initial grade was too low, we changed the strategy slightly for the next test, and perhaps again for the next test, continuing to make adjustments until we eventually reached what we considered an acceptable level of success.

Our teachers did their best, of course, to lead by example. They encouraged us to title, underline and date all our work, just as they did with their work on the board. They reminded us to review our notes once a week so that the information would stay fresh in our minds. They often suggested that we do the optional exercises in the textbook for extra practice. Later, in the corporate and industrial worlds many of us worked in, supervisors continued on exactly the same course.

But no one actually showed us what to do or how to do it — and so we didn't understand why we *should* do it. No one really explained how our brains work, how we learn, how we remember. Because, unfortunately, they honestly didn't know themselves.

But that excuse can't be used any more. We know plenty now! And so it's time for us to begin using our brains in a way that will help them operate at the kind of peak capacity that they're perfectly capable of.

So that's what this book is all about. Just as we know what kinds of food and exercise can help us perform better physically, we also now know what kinds of ideas and principles we need to help us perform better mentally.

When you're finished *The Big Learn*, I trust you'll have made the happy discovery that your brain is capable of much, much more than you ever thought possible.

THE BRAIN DOMAIN

It's not enough to have a good mind;
the main thing is to use it well.

René Descartes

01. What's The Problem?

Why don't we take advantage of the brain's full potential? What is it that prevents us from thinking, learning and communicating quickly and easily? The three most significant factors that regularly impede our performance are lack of interest, lack of attention and lack of effort.

LACK OF INTEREST

Maybe, when you were about seven years old and in primary school, you bounced out of bed every morning and ran enthusiastically off to school. Maybe, on those days, you just couldn't wait to sit at your desk for hours each day and learn, learn, learn.

But, if you're like most adults today, this kind of passionate energy petered out considerably over time. As an adolescent in high school, sitting at a desk hour after hour and day after day probably wasn't one of the greatest ways you could think of to spend your time. If you went on to the post-secondary level, it often might have seemed like a monumental task merely to get yourself to class and stay awake through the lectures.

Even if you've gone on to a satisfying career in a field you truly enjoy, it's most likely that you're faced pretty routinely with situations that can make paying attention a bit of a chore. Why? Because these circumstances are often *boring*.

Attending classes or meetings, writing essays or memos and reading textbooks or reports, to be sure, aren't the most fascinating experiences in the world.

And that's an absolutely gigantic problem. Lack of interest, probably more than any other factor, prevents us from learning well. Because the fact is that our brains love interesting information. In fact, they crave it! That's why we have very little trouble learning and remembering names and words and concepts that interest us.

When we're attracted to someone we'd very much like to meet and get to know better, we're quite likely to remember that person's name. When we read an article in a magazine that fascinates us, we'll probably be able to repeat its essential details later on. When we hear that X-brand widgets are on sale at Acme Supply Store for only $14.99 until next Friday, we can no doubt store that information in our memories pretty well. Why? Because these pieces of information interest us.

But boring stuff? Boring stuff bounces right off our heads. Our brains don't want to have *anything at all* to do with boring information. It's almost as if a strong steel cage is built around our heads, and its sole purpose is to prevent anything that's not intrinsically interesting from getting in. Naturally, this causes us problems.

LACK OF ATTENTION

When we don't attend to what we see or hear, it's dubious whether much actual learning will occur.

Now, I'm not referring so much to the individuals in the back corner of a room who are constantly talking to each other instead of listening, or those looking out the window or simply gazing abjectly into space, or those others doodling on pieces of paper instead of 'paying attention'.

What I mean is that our brains actually work too well to make paying attention easy. Surprisingly, perhaps, our brains are much too efficient and usually work far too rapidly to accommodate information that's so often presented to them, particularly through passive methods.

It's generally believed that our brains process information at a rate of between 1000 and 25000 words per minute. It's important, for a variety of reasons, to understand how this lowest limit of information-processing speed of around 1000 words per minute affects so much of what we do.

It's long been suggested by learning theorists that slowing down brain waves is conducive to enhanced learning achievement. Such research has led to the practice, in some circles, of using relaxation techniques or music to calm the brain down in order to improve its capacity to work and learn.

I'll admit that it took me quite some time myself to accept this kind of theory. Such a concept seemed too simple to be true — too illogical in terms of the academic research I was used to studying and, in fact, performing. But I've now both read about and personally witnessed plenty of success stories based on such ideas, so I'm more accepting of their worth.

The brain works at such an incredibly fast pace that it has difficulty processing day-to-day information that tends to travel, by comparison, at a turtle-like pace.

LACK OF EFFORT

Successful individuals are those people who learn faster, remember better and achieve more.

Many of us make the assumption that these people are blessed with innately superior abilities and stronger memory systems — better brains. But this simply isn't true. Most human beings are born with pretty good genes for memory, and neuroscientists say that our brains are capable of performing significantly better than was previously thought possible.

According to current research, we have the ability to perform at extraordinarily high levels, but what we must first understand, above all else, is that we should use our brains to try harder. Those who outperform the rest of us do exactly that. (Maybe that's what makes them so smart!)

Now, I'm not talking about a sweat-dripping-off-the-body kind of effort. I mean they simply think about learning situations well ahead of time. They prepare themselves mentally because they understand that learning won't occur magically on its own. Making an effort this way provides the brain with a foundation for learning. But, without that initial push, truly effective learning will quite simply not take place — at least, not very easily.

Getting ready to use our brains so that they'll be able to work at peak efficiency, then, requires an awareness of these three significant factors:

INTEREST

ATTENTION

EFFORT

BRAIN WAVES

02. The Passive Learning Debacle

In a landmark study performed many years ago, a psychologist named Dr. Hermann Ebbinghaus developed what he called the Curve of Forgetting, sometimes referred to as the Retention Curve. The subjects of Dr. Ebbinghaus' study were asked to memorize lists of information, usually nonsense words, which were initially unfamiliar to them. They learned these lists in a passive way, either by listening to someone repeating the 'words' or by simply reading and rereading them. Once they'd learned the information, they were tested at regular intervals — minutes, hours, days, weeks, even months later.

The results, as indicated in Figure 1 below, were disappointing to say the least. They were, in fact, quite shocking:

Fig. 1 • The Curve of Forgetting

What Dr. Ebbinghaus found was that, after passive learning, almost half of the information was forgotten *within about 20 minutes of reading or listening to it.* Close to 60% was forgotten within the first hour!

So what does this mean? Well, it means that, within an hour of leaving a room in which a meeting or a lecture has just taken place, most of the material learned passively has likely already been lost. It means that, almost as soon as you've finished a report or a textbook chapter you've just spent hours reading, you've probably already forgotten most of the content. In other words, passive learning doesn't work very well.

And the most discouraging aspect of this research? The original study was performed in 1885. (Not 1985. 1885!) Amazingly, we've known for well over 100 years that passive learning is an inefficient way to master information, yet we've done incredibly little to accept that fact and haven't done much to change our basic approach to the methods we use to learn.

This kind of research, by the way, has been carried out numerous times over the past century, and the results consistently echo the original Ebbinghaus study. In spite of this, we continue for the most part to train our children, once they've advanced past the primary grades in school, to be passive learners.

It's certainly no wonder then that, when they grow older and join the workplace as adults, their learning skills leave so much to be desired. Certainly, most individuals today are ill-equipped to cope with the greatest modern-day challenge of the data revolution that's been created by today's advancing technological juggernaut: information overload.

There is a cure, however, for this shortcoming in our
short-term memory systems, as illustrated in Figure 2.
It's called the Curve Of Remembering:

Fig. 2 • The Curve Of Remembering

According to this graph, if we learn actively and
take decent notes when first hearing or reading or
thinking about new material, all that will then be
required to keep this information at the forefront of our
memory system will be a quick review shortly after
learning it. A review session one day after learning the
information restores everything we'd lost. Following
that, to keep the material fresh, we'd take another look
the next day, once more a week later, and one more
time a month afterward.

Too much trouble? Hardly. Mere minutes of review
at regular intervals is far less inconvenient and takes
much less time than finding ourselves at a point, a
month after having been exposed to new learning,
where we've lost approximately 80% of what we
thought we'd already stored in our brains.

This is what successful thinkers do, and a great deal of research has shown that this is the kind of learning strategy that leads to significant savings in time, effort and energy.

My father was a teacher, and he was known for his ability to motivate even the most disinterested students to work to (and often beyond) what was considered to be their potential. He was always looking for ways to help them achieve that goal and would often pass on what he'd learned to me as well.

When I was in Grade 12, he must have come across the Curve of Remembering in an educational journal or, perhaps, at a conference he'd attended. I remember he and my mother sitting me down at the kitchen table one evening and explaining its simple concept to me.

They suggested to me that perhaps my academic performance at that time would improve considerably if I'd just take a bit of time at the end of each week and simply review the notes I'd taken over the course of the previous five school days. It wouldn't take much time, they assured me, and would probably bump up my marks significantly.

And I remember thinking: *What sweet people. They think I have notes!*

When I searched my schoolbag, of course, I couldn't find these notes they were referring to. Because I'd never been given much, if any, constructive notetaking training, I had no idea how to actively develop an effective system of recording new information as I was learning it. As a result, the only scraps of paper I could find in my knapsack were pretty much useless for me to review.

(I didn't want to hurt my parents' feelings, though. I knew their hearts were in the right place, so I assured them that I'd follow their advice, lock myself in my room every Friday night, and review, review, review!)

Of course, the result of blindly ignoring the substantial base of learning research that's been available to us, added to our profound lack of proper training in successful active learning strategies, is that most of us, later on, are simply overwhelmed by more information than we know how to manage.

Our brains, remember, process information between 1000 and 25000 words per minute. So let me explain what happens when we approach our two most common learning experiences — reading and listening — in a passive way.

READING

Let's say you're faced with some learning that requires reading 30 pages of fairly dry written material. And let's assume that, knowing this task will probably be somewhat onerous, you consider what you now know about your brain's information-processing rate and take measures that will slow your brain down to its minimal speed of 1000 WPM.

You start to read. Your eyes move across every line of print at the average adult reading speed of 250 WPM. At the appropriate moments, your fingers turn the pages. Your eyes continue to sweep gracefully across each line. Your fingers keep turning the pages. And after, let's say, one hour of this kind of sustained exercise in passive reading, you stop and realize that... *you have no idea what you've just read.*

Admit it. This has likely happened to you far more often than you'd probably care to acknowledge. Instead of comprehending the words and storing the concepts, your brain is often on automatic pilot while you read. In the example above, you've just spent 60 minutes doing what? Nothing, that's what.

Well, not nothing, really. Your brain *has* in fact been working. It's actually been thinking the whole time — about a conversation you had with a friend earlier in the day, about some family problems you're having, about a movie someone suggested you should watch, about a joke you were told earlier in the day, about what your plans are for the weekend, etc., etc., etc. What your brain was *not* thinking about too much, however, was the material you thought you were reading.

Why not? Some elementary mathematics provides the simple answer. When you subtract your reading rate of 250 WPM from your brain's slowest processing speed of 1000 WPM, you're left with 750 WPM of cognitive activity applied to information that's totally unrelated to what you were trying to read.

In other words, three quarters (75%!) of what you were thinking about while reading was dealing with completely foreign material — information, in all likelihood, that was more interesting than the text.

Of course, given the fact that most of us aren't even vaguely aware of the advantages of slowing down our brains to learn better in the first place, it's most probable that they're usually working at a much, much faster rate than 1000 WPM. And, obviously, the faster our brains are working, the less efficient our reading becomes.

Reading in a passive way, then, is largely a waste of time. Simply moving our eyes and turning pages most decidedly does *not* transfer information to our long-term memory systems. So the way most of us have been taught to read clearly doesn't work very well in real life.

LISTENING

Sadly, the act of passive listening is even less efficient than passive reading. The average person's rate of speech is around just 125 WPM. Subtract this speed from the slowest brain-processing rate of 1000 WPM and you'll understand that the passive listening that takes place in classrooms, in auditoriums, in offices, in meeting rooms and in conference halls has a very low probability of being effective.

As a professional speaker myself, I often joke that what I do for a living doesn't really work very well — that, at any particular moment in time, every single person in the room *(including myself while I'm speaking)* is thinking about something else. In fact, we're thinking about all sorts of things that have absolutely nothing to do with what I'm actually talking about at the time. Such is the power of the brain.

Standing in front of a group of people and simply talking to them can't possibly be very useful, then, unless the speaker and the participants engage in some form of active learning process. And active learning is definitely not what most of us are normally doing because, unfortunately, it's unlikely that we were ever trained to do so. See Figure 3 to better comprehend how much of our brains are actually paying attention when passively listening or reading:

125 WPM	250 WPM	1000 WPM	25000 WPM
LISTENING SPEED	READING SPEED	MINIMUM BRAIN SPEED	MAXIMUM BRAIN SPEED

Fig. 3 • Learning Speed vs. Brain Speed

It's true that the human brain is quite capable of processing large amounts of information at amazing rates of speed. But to genuinely focus our brains requires their conscious employment in suitably active processes. It's only then that the material can be both learned well and remembered later.

BRAIN WAVES

03. The Dilemma Of Memory

If you've ever taken a psychology course, you may remember learning that human beings are blessed with not one but two memory systems: short-term (called working memory) and long-term (called permanent memory).

Each system, alas, is ingrained with specific weaknesses that interfere with the way we use our brains when we try to process, learn and remember new information.

CAPACITY

Information first enters the short-term memory, the capacity of which is woefully limited. As psychologists will tell you, the Magic Number Of Memory is seven. In other words, once we try to place more than seven bits of information in our short-term memory systems, difficulties will arise.

Learning seven-digit numbers, then, is within the natural capabilities of short-term memory; learning ten-digit numbers is not. And once any list exceeds seven bits — seven digits, seven words, seven phrases, seven sentences, seven ideas, seven concepts — we'll begin to have problems.

Research suggests, in fact, that learning a list of ten items is 20 to 30 times more difficult than learning a list of seven. Our short-term memory systems are *always* full with seven bits of information. When a new bit of information is added, an old bit must necessarily be expelled.

And new bits of information are, of course, constantly entering the short-term memory system. Every time we think, hear, read, say, smell or touch something, new content finds its way in. And, every time that happens, old content is displaced. There's just no way around it; that's just the way the short-term memory system works.

This is not the case, however, with long-term memory, which has an absolutely huge storage capability. As a matter of fact, it's unlikely that any of us will ever fill even half of the long-term memory system's capacity. Even if we learn new things every single day and live to be 120 years old, our long-term memories will assuredly have plenty of space still available for information storage.

Our memory capacity far exceeds that of any computer yet designed, which is one of the reasons that Bill Gates, for one, calls the human brain one of the greatest mysteries of science.

PERSISTENCE

Just as memory capacity is a weakness of short-term memory and a strength of long-term memory, so is the life span (called persistence) of each bit of information.

If bits of old information are forced out of the short-term memory every time new material enters, and since new bits enter at a constant rate, there exists an extremely small window when information can make the passage from the short-term to the long-term system. Indeed, this life span is, on average, only about 30 seconds.

In other words, if we don't deliberately move new information within that brief time frame into long-term memory, it will quickly be displaced and forgotten.

This problem is particularly acute when it's related to traditionally passive learning experiences like reading and listening. In practical terms, this indicates that, unless we make an attempt to *do* something within approximately 30 seconds of new information entering short-term memory, we won't be able to recall it later.

For example, when we read material that we want to remember, we often won't be able to do so unless we consciously deal with it while it briefly resides in short-term memory. Likewise, when we listen to someone telling us something, we must also be aware of this limitation.

As with memory capacity, persistence is not a problem with long-term memory. Once information has been securely placed in long-term memory, it stays there forever. Although many find this difficult to believe and accept, it's a fact that long-term memory never loses information that's been stored there.

Here's a simple example: You leave home, get into your car and turn on the radio. A song you haven't heard for quite some time (let's say ten years) starts playing. While you used to hear this song regularly, you haven't listened to it or even consciously thought about it even once over the past decade.

So what happens almost as soon as the song starts playing? *You're singing along.* It's quite likely that, after only a few notes of music, the complete song has been lifted out of the recesses of your mind.

You remember the tune, the lyrics, when the drums will kick in, when and how the piece will end. Those initial notes act as memory triggers that bring the complete song back — after an apparent absence of ten long years — into your present-day conscious memory.

So far as capacity and persistence are concerned, then, the two systems are at odds; what are strengths in long-term memory are weaknesses in short-term memory. A similar situation exists when it comes to the processes of input and output, but in reverse. This time, the short-term strengths are the long-term weaknesses.

INPUT

Information enters the short-term memory quickly — in fact, almost immediately. It takes no time at all for new material to make its way into our working memory system. It's a quick and easy process.

Not so, however, with long-term memory. Loading newly learned material takes time. Because of this, the main reason most of us are often reluctant to enter into new learning situations is that we fear the amount of time that will be required to master the new knowledge. Experience tells us that traditional methods of moving information into long-term memory — particularly memorizing through the process of repetition — are painstakingly slow.

This weakness of our long-term memory system often prevents us from approaching new learning with any kind of enthusiasm. In a world already rife with time-consuming tasks, adding another such chore to the mix is just not something we view as desirable.

OUTPUT

Information stored in short-term memory is easily accessible. The one proviso here is, of course, that only a small amount of material resides there, and it lingers for only a short period of time. It's quite possible, though, to find one of the seven bits of information easily so long as we access it sometime during its brief 30-second existence in the short-term memory system.

On the other hand, information stored in long-term memory can be very difficult to find. Its enormous capacity can make its bloated filing system somewhat complicated. Because every single fragment of material ever stored in long-term memory remains there, trying to find one of those small bits can be a daunting task.

Unfortunately, we tend to rely on a particularly ineffective method of storing knowledge. That is, we view our brains as big filing cabinets. When we read something, for instance, and want to remember a specific fact, we make what is commonly known as a 'mental note' and place it in one of the filing cabinet drawers.

Some mental notes go in one specific drawer, while others are stored in alternate drawers. We do this regularly, continuously adding snippets of conversation, jokes we hear, songs we listen to, material we read, sights we see, scents we smell, etc.

Later on, when we want to recall what's been stored, we open up one of the drawers to find what we're looking for. But there are many, many drawers and — because we tend not to use any particular system for filing information — we're usually not exactly sure which drawer to search. And that creates a big problem.

Of course, even if we do access the correct filing cabinet drawer, we then quickly discover something else: *there are no file folders.* So now we're faced with rummaging through the equivalent of millions upon millions of tiny, unrelated, confetti-sized pieces of paper, each one noting a particular fact or name or number or idea or concept or thought.

This explains why we read a test question and are well aware that we've studied the material and stored the particular piece of information we need to answer the question — but then realize, with a sinking feeling, that it seems impossible to find it.

It also explains why, when dealing with a particular issue at a meeting, we can't always remember the specific question we wanted to ask or the suggestion we wanted to make. It's the reason we often have information 'on the tip of the tongue' but can't actually say the word.

SO MUCH FOR MENTAL NOTES!

BRAIN WAVES

THE AMAZING BRAIN

*Creative minds have always been known
to survive any kind of bad training.*

Anna Freud

04. The Successful Brain

Way back in the 1970s, in a groundbreaking book called *Use Your Head*, Tony Buzan lamented the fact that so many people remained skeptical about the potential of the human brain. If our brains were so powerful, these people reasoned, then why was it that so few of us seemed to use them very well?

To address their skepticism, Buzan conducted a survey to find out what those folks had actually been taught about the brain's potential. The following are a few of the questions he asked:

*In school, were you taught anything about
your brain and how understanding its functions
could help you learn, memorize, think, etc.?*

Were you taught anything about how your memory functions?

*Anything about the ranges of study techniques and
how they can be applied to different disciplines?*

*Anything about motivation, how it affects your abilities
and how you can use it to your advantage?*

Anything about thinking?

At least 95% of the respondents answered "no" to each of the questions. It would seem, then, that the reason we don't use our brains better isn't necessarily because our brains don't work very well.

Rather, the reason we don't use them anywhere close to their potential is more likely because we haven't been taught how they work or shown what to do with them. What Mr. Buzan discovered in his survey was a sad commentary on how we were trained to use our brains, but it's even sadder that — so many years after his original survey — so little has changed.

In the mid-1980s, the United States Committee For Economic Development chose to study what it takes to get ahead. After administering a survey to over 400 large businesses, 6000 small businesses and 500 colleges and universities, it compiled and published the following list of five characteristics essential for success, in order of importance:

1. knowing how to learn
2. striving to work well
3. being able to set priorities
4. using problem-solving skills
5. having the ability to communicate

It's really no surprise that knowing how to learn is the #1 characteristic on the list. There is overwhelming evidence from a variety of sources that learning to learn is at the crux of personal growth and achievement, yet very little has been done to address the problem.

In the 1940s, an American educator named Edgar Dale began studying the issue of how we learn, and later researchers developed and revised his work, resulting in the Cone of Learning, as shown in Figure 4:

10% OF WHAT WE READ — reading — PASSIVE

20% OF WHAT WE HEAR — hearing words

30% OF WHAT WE SEE — looking at pictures

watching a movie

looking at an exhibit

50% OF WHAT
WE HEAR & SEE — watching a demonstration

seeing it done on location

70% OF WHAT
WE SAY — participating in a discussion

giving a talk

doing a dramatic presentation

90% OF WHAT
WE SAY & DO — simulating a real experience — ACTIVE

doing the real thing

Fig. 4 • Cone of Learning

According to their analysis, when we choose reading as our preferred learning technique, as we so often do (as most of us have been *trained* to do), we tend to remember only 10% of the content.

Hearing someone explain information to us, on the other hand, doubles our ability to recall material later —— but our learning capacity is still stuck at a measly efficiency level of only 20%. When we have the opportunity to see material expressed in a visual format, our ability to learn and remember increases to 30%.

A combination of the second and third levels of the Cone of Learning, hearing and seeing, boosts our learning potential to 50%.

A few years ago, I was presented with a prime example of the potential of our learning power at this particular level. Here's the story:

A young man in his late teens approached me, asking for advice about his educational future. Four years prior to our talk, he'd taken his considerable height and impressive athletic skills to a local high school renowned for its outstanding basketball program.

By the end of Grade 11, he was a prime member of the school's junior team which hadn't lost a game in three years of league play. He was being scouted already by well-known colleges. This guy loved his school, and his excellence on the basketball court was reflected academically in the classroom. Early in Grade 12, however, he suffered a knee injury that knocked him off the team and essentially ended his athletic career at school.

And how that affected his performance as a student! By the end of the year, his academic situation was bleak. Without the motivation that had been provided by his athletic prowess, his marks and his attitude had dropped to a dangerously low level. He skipped classes, copied other students' notes and spent little time studying. A week before final exams, he suddenly decided that he wanted to apply to a college program, acceptance to which would be determined solely by his mark on his upcoming English exam.

So I asked him how his prospects looked. His reply: "Well, we've been studying Shakespeare and reading Hamlet. I haven't read the play, I've skipped at least half the classes, I borrowed some of my friends' assignments to hand in, I don't like the teacher much, and she doesn't seem to care for me at all. In a nutshell, I'm barely scraping by."

I remember that day very clearly. I looked up at my son (my own flesh and blood!), Dan, and said: "Well, for starters, I think you'd better read the play!" His response: "What good would that do? It's like Martian or something! And I haven't been to enough of the classes to get the drift of the story." So my next suggestion was for him to buy the condensed, annotated version of the play sold by a large bookstore chain. His response to this idea: "No way! It's too much to read, and it costs too much! I don't have the time or the money!" It was at this point, I believe, that I threw up my arms and, rightly or wrongly, walked away and gave up on the kid.

On his own, though (because he did, in fact, have a pretty good brain inside his head), he devised a plan that he felt suited his particular personal agenda. He went to a video store around the corner and rented the movie, Hamlet (starring that great Shakespearian actor himself: Mel Gibson) and, the night before the big exam, watched the movie twice, back to back. Three hours of 'studying'.

And the result? He scored the highest mark in the class. And, miraculously (at least to me at the time), he gained entrance into the college program of his choice.

So I guess the moral of this story, based on my own family's personal experience, is this: *Seeing* and *hearing* information simultaneously is quite likely to boost learning power significantly.

Now, I'm not suggesting that we all stop reading and simply start watching movies instead. Imagine what would have happened if my son had read the play, attended all the classes, asked plenty of questions, reviewed his notes — and *then* watched the movie for review the night before the exam. The kid would have been considered a genius!

Nevertheless, the 'strong' students who had studied the material the traditional way, the way they'd been trained to learn — primarily by reading and rereading (at the least efficient level of 10%) — achieved far poorer results on the exam than the 'weak' student whose brain hung onto at least 50% of the information that he'd both seen and heard from watching the movie. He remembered what Mel Gibson looked like, what he was wearing, his facial expressions, his tone of voice, his physical surroundings from one scene to the next. A stellar example of the truth and wisdom of the Cone of Learning!

For an even more powerful learning experience, the research indicates that saying things aloud, explaining information to someone else, locks material into our brains at an efficiency level of 70%. Ironically, many of our schools, with perfectly good intentions, have initiated various kinds of mentoring programs, engaging bright students to tutor their weaker peers in an effort to help them improve their grades. (We often take the same course of action in the workplace when we partner highly proficient personnel with less accomplished employees in training contexts.)

And what happens? The competent ones get much stronger because they're the ones doing the explaining while the weak ones make only modest gains because they're the ones doing the listening — just as the Cone of Learning suggests.

Finally, at the base of the Cone, at an astonishing success rate of 90%, is saying and doing. In other words, our total learning capacity is close to its maximum when we actually participate in the process.

The obvious deduction to be drawn from the Cone of Learning is that active use of our brains leads to superior learning experiences, while passive involvement doesn't — a sobering fact that should be heeded by those currently smitten by the rather euphemistically named 'learner-centred' movement which espouses individual learning with the assistance of manuals, DVDs and computer-assisted programs.

Such a conclusion affirms the intrinsic value of active learning and suggests an indictment of the way most of us have been educated and the way we continue to train and be trained. After all, how did we spend most of our time in school if not reading and listening — the categorically *least effective* methods on the scale?

Long after the Cone Of Learning was first published, in a 1995 survey at a large Canadian community college, over 4000 students were asked to list their primary concerns as post-secondary students. Here's how they responded:

Reading Skills:	9%
Writing Skills:	18%
Academic Ability:	20%
Math Skills:	25%
Study Skills:	48%

There it is again. Almost half the students weren't sure how to study! They had some concerns, too, with reading, writing and math — but at least we make a concerted effort to teach those skills to them. But how much of our time and resources and money do we allocate to teaching people how to learn?

The attrition rate at colleges and universities is woeful. Some students drop out because of financial duress, others because of personal issues, and still others because they lack appropriate literacy and numeracy skills.

But, according to studies like the one just cited, the primary reason so many students fail to make the grade at this level of education is because they've never been properly taught how to learn. It's little wonder, then, that they're a bit mystified when confronted with the independent learning trend. How on earth will they be able to learn on their own if no one has explained basic learning principles to them?

So what exactly is going on here? Many years ago, the Buzan questionnaire suggested that we had a problem and, more recently, a major American government report revealed similar results. Yet today's most current surveys seem to indicate that little has been done to correct the fact that we continue to deny people the basic knowledge they need to achieve success.

Oh, by the way, it's actually been a very, very long time that we've been aware of this problem. And we didn't really need to spend years of research and millions of dollars to discover its root cause, either. I wonder if you've heard this ancient Chinese proverb that's centuries old:

I hear... and I forget.
I see... and I remember.
I do... and I understand.

Time for us to get working on our brains, huh?

BRAIN WAVES

05. Brain Growth

We refer to the human brain as 'gray matter'. Gray, being the dullest of colours, is generally associated with all things common and dreary, and perhaps that's why some of us have made the unfortunate mistake of thinking that the brain is a cheerless organ.

Of course, the complete opposite is true — and in spades. In fact, the human brain is colourful, dynamic, creative and exciting. It's lively and entertaining and electrifying and potent.

Bill Gates, founder of Microsoft and, by any measure, a very intelligent and successful individual, used to write a syndicated column published in newspapers around the world. In his column, he replied to letters and fielded questions, usually computer-related, from his readers.

Early in 1997, one writer asked: "If you could find the answer to just one question, what would you ask?" His answer surely surprised many readers, who most probably expected his answer to deal with the world of high-information technology.

Here's what he wrote: *"I'd like to understand how the human brain works. If there were an ultimate answer machine, that's the question I'd ask. I'm in awe of the brain and its ability to learn."*

Given all the tremendous changes and challenges in the world today, what fascinates Mr. Gates the most is not the hardware and software that has helped to make him so wealthy and powerful, but an organic device that's been with us from the beginning.

And barely a week goes by these days without more newly discovered information about the inner workings of the brain appearing in our local newspapers, national magazines, television news reports and websites.

In the 1950s, when neuroscience was very much in its infancy, brain researchers came to the startling conclusion that we don't consciously use 100% of our brain's capacity. At the time, they thought they'd discovered (and were discouraged to think) that we probably use only about half of it. In the 1960s and 1970s, newer information seemed to support the theory that we probably use only about 20%. In the 1980s, that was pared down to 10%. One tenth of our brains!

Ever since then, it seems that every subsequent report that's been written has contained information that suggests that these prior predictions were merely conservative guesses. One article I read some time ago, for instance, suggested that we actively use only 5-6%, and then, just a short while later, another one hinted that it was more like 2-3%. I remember thinking, after reading in a journal article that I probably use only 1% of my brain: *Enough! That's as low as I'm prepared to go!*

But some researchers today seem to believe that the percent of our brains that we have conscious access to could be as low as .01%. Or less.

So what's this mean to the average person on the street? Plenty. It means that the incredible gains being made in the field of brain research will have significant impact on our lives. As scientists learn more and more about how we think and feel and learn, this new knowledge is bound to give us the ability to use our brains much more efficiently in the very near future.

Another discovery made back in the 1960s concerned the number of different patterns the billions of individual neurons in the brain could collectively make. Researchers surmised that that number was something like 10^{800}.

Now, to get a handle on how large this number actually is, consider that the number of atoms in the universe is around 10^{34}. Atoms are almost the smallest particles we know of — there are billions of them in the tips of each of our fingers — and the universe is pretty well the biggest entity we can even imagine. Yet there are countlessly more connections being made inside one human brain at any particular moment in time than we have atoms in the universe.

If you find these kinds of numbers quite unbelievable or, perhaps, simply too difficult to comprehend because of their magnitude, consider the following example:

As you're reading these words on this page, the most advanced and complex 'computer' in existence, your brain, is processing an incredible number of electrical impulses prompted by light bouncing off 14 million colour sensors and 200 million black and white sensors. This happens every time you read the printed word.

And this example: *Richard Restak, M.D., author of The Brain, suggests that one human brain can store more information than we have collected in all the libraries in the world put together.*

And this example: *According to The Brain Book, by Peter Russell, the capacity of the brain's memory systems is on the order of a quadrillion (1000 million million) bits of information.*

No wonder Bill Gates is so fascinated with the operation of the human brain! To say that the achievements of the most powerful computer in existence today pales in comparison to the capability of the human brain is a monumental understatement.

In 1996, IBM challenged Gary Kasparov, the world chess champion at the time, to a match. Mr. Kasparov, one of the greatest chess masters in history, relished the opportunity and accepted. Now, I've played chess often enough to know that it's not a game for the weak-hearted or feeble-minded. Given my own difficulties with the game, to be quite frank, I found it hard to believe that the owner of a three-pound brain would stand any chance at all of beating a supercomputer programmed specifically to play chess.

But Gary Kasparov won the match handily, and most of the world (with the exception, perhaps, of the IBM computer programming team) breathed a collective sigh of relief, reassured that humans were still, in fact, smarter than machines. Not to be deterred, though, IBM requested a rematch to take place the following year.

In the spring of 1997, the historic match was played. This time, IBM introduced a chess-playing computer known as Deep Blue, a six-foot-five monster weighing 3000 pounds with the capacity to analyze 50 billion chess positions in the three minutes allowed between moves and capable of planning 14 moves ahead.

The human won the first game. The machine won the second. The third game was a draw. So was the fourth. And the fifth.

And then it happened: Deep Blue won the sixth game to defeat the world's human chess champion. And people around the globe started to believe what they'd been seeing in all those futuristic movies — that what lies in wait for us is our inevitable submission to a master race of mechanical masters.

But rest assured: that's not what it meant at all. Once the ballyhoo had died down, the doom and gloom discussions in the media began to be replaced by much more positive and reassuring stories. One computer expert after another (even the ones from IBM) explained to us that Deep Blue wasn't even 'intelligent' by any human standard and that the chess win had absolutely nothing at all to do with what's generally referred to as artificial intelligence. The computer, to be sure, didn't have a mind of its own.

I'll let Bill Gates have the last word on this issue. In his syndicated newspaper column (July 1997), this is what he said to help us understand what had actually transpired:

"The victory has little significance... The computer that was used to beat Kasparov didn't figure out how to play chess; it was told by some people to do some mechanical, numeric comparisons. The machine didn't recognize any patterns; it didn't gain any knowledge by playing those chess games in any way, shape or form. It just performed rote calculations blindingly fast... It does one thing: it plays chess. It can't even play checkers or balance a chequebook, let alone appreciate humour or reason with a child... Gary Kasparov's brain can play checkers, translate Russian into English and rapidly cope with new circumstances. It can also beat Deep Blue in chess some of the time. That's awesome."

Let's stop worrying about computers catching up to us, then, and concentrate instead on learning to use our own brains better. Research suggests that our brains have the potential to work far better and much more capably than we ever thought possible.

Even if we do, in fact, use only a fraction of the brain's capacity, we're now in a position to take what we know and turn that information to practical use. Neuroscientists are relentlessly hot on the trail of possibilities. Their quest is not only to analyze how brains operate, but also to assimilate what they learn and suggest better ways to use them.

You may remember a movie from several years ago called *Rain Man*. Tom Cruise was one of its stars, and Dustin Hoffman played the role of an autistic savant — plagued by autism, yet blessed with genius.

While his autism caused serious problems that very much affected his day-to-day life and prevented his ability to live what most of us would call a normal life, his seemingly super intelligence (the 'savant' part) was a gift. He seemed able to take his brain to heights regular mortals weren't nearly capable of.

When he visited Las Vegas and stopped in at the casinos, he was not only able to count cards, but could also almost instantly figure out odds and probabilities of winning and losing. This led to almost unheard-of success at the gaming tables, much to his crooked brother's delight.

When a box of toothpicks dropped and broke open on a restaurant floor, spilling its contents on the floor, he immediately counted them and figured out how many toothpicks were missing.

Just think what we could do if given access to that kind of brain! Wouldn't it be great if *our* brains worked that way, too? Well, perhaps scientists will soon be able to help us do just that.

Autistic savants, after all, have brains inside their heads just as we do, but their amazing brains can make instantaneous calculations and remember words and facts and numbers incredibly well. But autistic savants seem to use theirs a bit differently than we use ours. Perhaps, once researchers understand what those specific differences are, we may be able to apply this knowledge to achieve similar kinds of results.

Of course, as I've said, we're already quite aware of a number of strategies that can improve the way we use our brains. Thanks, in part, to George H. Bush's presidential proclamation that the 1990s be designated The Decade Of The Brain, scientists have been hard at work ever since, using increasingly powerful new technologies to examine brains.

One of the most interesting magazine articles I read in that decade, *Building A Better Brain* by Daniel Golden, appeared as the cover story of the July 1994 issue of *Life* magazine. The article covered a wide range of brain-related topics, but one of its most fascinating stories concerned the School Sisters of Notre Dame, head-quartered in Mankato, Minnesota, and their partici-pation in some research called The Nun Study.

The nearly 700 sisters in this order became the largest group of brain donors in the world, and researchers are fascinated both by their longevity and by their apparent resistance to the normal brain problems common to the general population.

The article went on to suggest that, because these particular nuns insist on living intellectually challenging lives, their brains display a remarkable ability to continue growing stronger — even when they're in their 90s. The key to their success is what I like to call The Dendrite Story, and it has huge implications to how we use our brains — in the classroom, in the workplace and in our personal lives.

The human brain, remember, is made up of billions and billions of brain cells called neurons. As Golden's article explains:

Each neuron contains at one end threadlike appendages called axons, which send signals to other nearby neurons. At the other end of the neuron are similar threadlike appendages called dendrites, which receive messages from nearby cells.

Experiments have shown that increased intellectual activity, at any age, induces the neurons to branch out like the roots of a growing tree. As each cell grows larger branches, improved communication among them increases, leading to the brain's superior ability to perform tasks and even modify its behaviour when confronted with complex challenges.

The Sisters of Mankato work hard at staying both physically healthy and mentally active by continuing to do brain-challenging jobs far past the traditional retirement age — by learning new vocabulary, playing card games, solving puzzles — and they continue to grow new dendrite branches well into old age.

The following is an example of what different brain cells can look like:

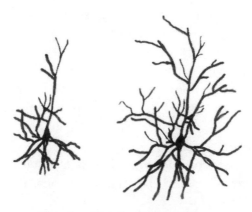

Fig. 5 • The Dendrite Story

On the brain cell at the left, you see some dendrite growth caused by normal thinking processes. At the right is a cell from a brain that's intentionally been presented with above-average stimulation. Note the latter cell's much more extensive dendrite branches.

To encourage superior dendrite development, then, it's important that we stimulate our brains with challenging mental tasks. Rather than accept the humdrum normality of what the average human brain is introduced to each day, we'd be wise to arouse our brain cells, pushing them to perform at higher levels. Through this kind of process, we'll have the opportunity to make ourselves smarter.

Growing our dendrites bigger and better, though, isn't necessarily a matter of forcing ourselves to do things which seem punitive. We can make our brains work better in a variety of ways, many of them quite enjoyable. For example, continuing to so some kind of work, especially work we like to do, is important.

Many of us know people who retire from their jobs and simply sit in front of the TV day in and day out. These people will lose some of their mental abilities quickly, given the attendant lack of stimulation. Others we know retire and use their brains in brand new ways — by taking up new hobbies, enrolling in night-school courses, engaging in volunteer work or traveling to places they've never been to before.

Doing puzzles, whether they be of the crossword, sudoku or jigsaw variety, can also ignite dendrite growth. So can playing bridge instead of bingo.

It's the *process* of learning that's good for the brain. Learning a new language, for example, will help form connections inside our brains that didn't exist before, but setting arbitrary time limits — some magazine advertisements implore us to learn a new language in as little as three weeks! — isn't the point.

Taking our time, even if it takes years rather than weeks, ensures that our brains will have time to create new connections and grow stronger. Even something as simple as leading an active social life improves brain function, because interacting with different people is bound to introduce us to things we didn't know before.

We'd be wise to heed an old saying that goes like this: *We don't stop playing because we grow old. We grow old because we stop playing.*

Young children's brains thrive and flourish every single day, largely because they spend so much of their time playing. Unfortunately, as we age, we tend to forget the value of playing with lots of different kinds of 'toys', and this, in turn, curbs the kind of dendrite growth we continue to be capable of producing.

So that's The Dendrite Story. Is it relevant to us? You bet it is. In fact, knowing simple ways to stimulate dendrite growth can make immeasurable differences to everything we do at school, at work and at home.

Understanding the powerful impact on our brains that new, different and interesting experiences can make will have an immediate impact on how we live, learn and communicate. In fact, it truly affects every single aspect of our lives.

BRAIN WAVES

06. Balancing Your Brain

Much has been written and discussed in recent years about the idea that the human brain isn't just a single entity, but an organ comprised of two distinct sides with a narrow passageway connecting the two. While not always very well understood, this left side/right side issue has now entered the realm of popular culture to the extent that it regularly appears in newspapers, television shows, movies and advertising. (A beer commercial on TV once took us into the right side of a young man's brain. Apparently, there are *parties* going on over there!)

As it turns out, the two sides of our brains process completely diverse kinds of information. While the left side deals with logic, for instance, the right side is much more creative. Figure 6 below presents a simple representation of the differences between left and right brain functions:

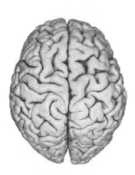

LOGIC	CREATIVITY
REASON	RHYTHM
MATH	IMAGERY
READING	DREAMS
WRITING	EMOTION
LANGUAGE	SYMBOLS
ANALYSIS	SYNTHESIS

Fig. 6 • Left Brain vs. Right Brain

This is a bit simplistic, I know, but here's one way to look at it:

THE LEFT SIDE IS LIKE
THE MOST BORING MEETING
YOU'VE EVER ATTENDED.

THE RIGHT SIDE IS LIKE
THE BEST PARTY
YOU'VE EVER BEEN TO!

Now, I realize that this kind of representation is unfair to the left side of the brain. After all, it's quite true that we'd hardly be able to get by without left-brain functions. In fact, a tremendous amount of what we do in school, with its emphasis on the three Rs, is based on left-brain learning.

The workplace, too, thrives on the same kinds of functions, often for good reason. But I'm illustrating the differences in this way in an effort to counteract mainstream society's almost exclusive and unwavering devotion to the value of the left side of the brain.

We live in an extremely left-brain culture. In truth, Western Civilization certainly holds concepts like logic, reason and analysis in intensely high regard. It's no coincidence that so many successful individuals hold their positions because of their left-brain abilities. It would, in fact, be difficult to attain leadership positions in most corporations, institutions and organizations without having demonstrably strong left-brain skills.

But that's not necessarily such a good thing for them — nor for the rest of us.

What it means is that our lives are often controlled by those who tend to show a somewhat muted regard for the functions of the right side of the brain. Yet it's the right side that motivates and invigorates us!

Focusing on left-side characteristics, indeed, helps provide society with rules and regulations that are generally considered essential in a civilized and technologically advanced society. It allows us to read and write and balance our chequebooks, to make the laws and run the banks and preside over our institutions. But ignoring the right-side properties of our brains can seriously prevent us from truly under-standing what makes human beings tick.

Some researchers have gone so far as to imply that our brains work best when we're happy, and that they operate at peak performance when they're working in tandem with our hearts. And, since issues that we associate with our hearts are primarily represented by functions of the right side of the brain, it follows that strong right-side skills will actually improve the work done by the left side that we value so much.

Now, some might suggest it's actually a very good thing that our society's most influential people are *not* predominantly right-brain thinkers — surmising that artists and musicians and inventors, for instance, probably wouldn't make such great presidents and bankers and judges. But that's not exactly what I'm getting at here.

Modern brain research indicates that strengthening the right side of the brain actually contributes to a direct improvement of the functioning of the left side of the brain.

So it's a *balanced* brain that we should be striving for. Unquestionably, the greatest minds in history haven't been individuals who simply had a powerful command of just one side of the brain. Even those people we usually associate with outstanding achievements in the fields of mathematics and language weren't purely one-dimensional (or one-sided) thinkers.

On the contrary, Albert Einstein — arguably the greatest mathematical mind of the twentieth century — played the violin, trusted his dreams and claimed to think in pictures and images first, and words and numbers last. Winston Churchill, known so much for his facility with language skills, very often spent his personal time with brush in hand, creating landscape paintings. Mohandas Ghandi, a renowned political leader, meditated daily to clarify his thoughts.

So it appears that most truly great thinkers use *both* sides of their brains to produce the kind of balanced-brain thinking that transcends the accomplishments of ordinary mortals.

It's a sad fact that, as we age, we tend to devalue the powers of the right side of the brain. Babies are born with two sides of the brain that work quite happily and constructively together. They learn about language and counting, for example, through play. When they get a little bit older, they continue to learn more complicated concepts with the help of the right side of the brain.

Imagine how long it would take them to learn the alphabet if they simply repeated the 26 letters in a monotone over and over and over. Instead, it's the accompanying tune and its rhythm that entrenches the alphabet so quickly and easily into young minds.

When children first start going to school, we refer to them as 'sponges' who soak up learning. Certainly, they learn an astonishing amount of knowledge and information in a very short time while enrolled in the primary grades. Well, perhaps that's because they use their brains the way brains work best, with the left and right sides cooperating with each other.

But then the trouble starts. As these children move from the primary to the junior grades, the adults in charge start taking a strange tack. They begin to abandon balanced-brain learning and increasingly choose to mould these young minds with left-brain teaching and left-brain learning techniques.

In spite of the fact that these young children learned the alphabet with relative ease, thanks to the addition of right-brain processes (music and rhythm) to the initial left-brain task, we teach slightly older ones the multiplication tables using purely left-brain techniques.

Rather than take the time to teach the times tables in a creative way, we insist instead that the poor kids repeat the numbers ad infinitum, copying them out day after day, with some kind of new-found misguided belief that logic and reason alone will lead to success.

And, sure, the children eventually do manage to lodge the times tables inside their long-term memories. But why take such a laborious left-brain route when the previously used balanced-brain strategies had been proven to work so well? While music certainly isn't the only right-brain trait that helps lead us to improved learning and thinking, many studies have proven that it's one of the most beneficial right-brain ways to supercharge the left brain's potential.

Researchers at the University of California at Irvine, for instance, have found that children who take regular music lessons achieve higher scores on math and reading tests. Some studies suggest, too, that students who play classical music in the background while studying generally receive higher grades on tests.

Hopefully, this kind of research will lead, in the near future, to changes in the way we both teach children and show them how to learn. With the rate of change clipping along at ever-increasing speed, it's essential that we do just that. Dr. Willard Daggett, a Director with the International Centre for Leadership & Education, once famously said that "the world our kids are going to live in is changing four times faster than our schools." So it's high time we addressed this issue.

But this is hardly just a matter for the schools. As adults, we already live in a changed and ever-changing world. In order to not only keep up but also to continue moving ahead, it's of paramount importance that we take new lessons about the brain and start putting them into practice.

One of the ways we can do that is to determine which side of our brain is dominant and then work to strengthen the weaker side. Becoming balanced-brain thinkers will serve us well in the workplace, for instance, where an immediate impact will be made on just about everything we do there, including the way we communicate, train, sell goods and services, develop marketing strategies, advertise and provide customer service — to name just a few examples.

Can we use our brains more successfully? Sure we can — by working to balance our brains.

BRAIN WAVES

07. The Perfect Brain Environment

I have to say I'm absolutely convinced that the perfect brain environment is the Grade 2 classroom. Imagine you're in one right now. What do you see as you look around the room? I imagine you're seeing many pictures — *big pictures* — and lots of colours — *bright colours*. Something else you notice at the front of the room, I'll bet, are the letters of the alphabet printed across the top of the blackboard with *illustrations* beside each of the letters.

How about anything overhead? You might see mobiles hanging from the ceiling. If you see words and numbers, they're large and they're associated with *graphics* and *images*. The desks are pushed together so that the children have an opportunity for *social interaction* during the day.

There's likely an area set aside where the children can sit on the floor, comfy on small pieces of carpet or cushions. Lots of reading material with *illustrations* and other *pictures* to look at. *Activity centres, toys* and *games*. There are generous-sized windows, and the curtains are almost always open. On warm summer days, primary school teachers sometimes take their pupils outside the school building where they'll learn just as well as they would indoors. Probably better.

Have you ever wondered why your work environment doesn't look something like that? Take a look at the italicized words above. You'll notice that all these words represent functions of the right side of the brain.

To be sure, the children in the room are there to learn all sorts of left-brain things. They're certainly learning words and numbers, language and math, reason and logic, reading and writing, calculating and analyzing. But the way those concepts are presented to them is via the other side of the brain. And it works. The kids learn things. Lots of things.

Now, in your mind's eye, replace that Grade 2 scene with a Grade 4 classroom. Notice any changes? You probably see that the words and the numbers seem smaller in size. The colours aren't quite so bright. There aren't as many pictures. The room seems neater and more organized somehow. Maybe the desks are now in rows instead of being joined together. There's no separate place to sit on the floor and not so many toys lying around. The books look less interesting.

Now try Grade 6, Grade 8, Grade 10 and Grade 12. A college classroom. A university lecture theater. A corporate training room. A hotel conference facility.

What you've just done is taken a guided tour from the right side of the brain to the left side of the brain. You've traveled from an area where natural learning experiences take place quite easily to a room where learning seems more formal and increasingly forced. This methodical and intentional shift away from a balanced-brain environment to a much more left-brain environment stifles, even retards, our performance at school and on the job more than most people imagine.

You know, many Grade 2 children actually love going to school. They bounce out of bed in the morning, truly looking forward to getting to their classrooms. Very often, they want to be the first ones there!

Most Grade 2 children like their teacher. And the teacher likes them. Hallelujah, let's get out there and learn some new stuff!

Of course, once in the classroom, these youngsters sometimes get bored. Their minds drift, just as ours do. But, when they stop concentrating on what the teachers are saying, what happens in that magnificent space inside their heads?

Well, they learn other things, that's what happens. The bored children look around the room and see, on the wall over here, the leaf rubbings they did last week: *There's a maple leaf, a willow leaf, an oak leaf.* And, on the wall over there, some numbers added together: *Oh, 4 plus 3 is 7 — not 12 like I was thinking.* Up above, the solar system mobiles are hanging from the ceiling: *The sun's in the middle, then Mercury and Venus and Earth and...*

Looking through the big windows, they watch some birds fighting over some scraps of food and learn something about wildlife. After reading time, sitting on the floor where they share some stories with their friends, they'll go outside to look at bugs in the ravine next to the schoolyard. After all: *It's a beautiful day! Why waste it inside?*

In Grade 4, though, there's not quite so much to entertain their minds when they drift. In Grade 6, they sometimes look outside and wonder what they're doing stuck indoors. By Grade 8, they're often waking up in the morning, thinking: *I don't think I feel well enough to go to school today.*

By the time our young people are ready to enter high school, the left-brainers have pretty well had their way with them.

At that point, learning by using a balanced-brain approach hardly even seems an option any more, other than maybe in the Art or Drama or Gym classes which, lamentably, are usually the first to suffer when school budgets are trimmed.

Colleges and universities can be even more impersonal. Students, for the most part, are now encouraged to learn on their own. The sad thing is that they've been almost totally indoctrinated with left-brain learning strategies that are the most boring, time-consuming, frustrating and aggravating ways to learn.

Shamefully, we frequently train our youth to use their brains in a manner that's quite opposite to the way their brains learn best, just as we ourselves were trained. While the Grade 2 child looks around the room, learning new information easily, the older student takes a glance around the room and sees... what? Concrete blocks. Colourless walls. No view. No fun.

And what about the workplace that's waiting after graduation? More bad news, right?

(Here's a case in point: I once delivered a series of workshops to an organization whose employees were stationed in small, colourless cubicles. Not only were there no windows to provide a view of the outside world, but the company had a policy that prohibited its workers from displaying anything on the walls that surrounded them. I suppose the theory was that the workers would focus on their jobs better without any unnecessary distractions.)

So what happened to the concept of the happy brain? The one that works better when it's stimulated by diverse and interesting stimuli?

A friend of mine once worked for a multinational corporation and had the opportunity to visit a cutting-edge office design firm to get some ideas for his company's planned office renovation. He came back totally jazzed about what he'd seen.

Here's what caught his attention and made him a believer: huge windows with great views for everyone to enjoy, separate work stations shared by whomever needed them at any particular time, individual music players to suit personal tastes, a full-service kitchen in the centre of the work area, comfortable sitting areas to relax and share ideas informally.

The design firm practiced what it preached, too, encouraging its own employees to enjoy the work environment, even inviting friends and family to drop by, so as to avoid the kind of cubicle-world, formal surroundings common to many large company offices. The employees responded by often working late, being more productive and developing a passionate loyalty to their organization. My friend was very impressed.

But his left-brained boss wasn't. In fact, he wouldn't even listen to the argument that happy workers make better workers. He didn't even stop to consider the effect that such an environment might have on how his employees' brains worked. So he nixed the concept. Score yet another point for the left-brainers.

Ask architects about the two most desirable features that make an environment livable, and here's what they'll tell you: *space* and *light*. Ask interior designers how to create an atmosphere conducive to serenity and creative thought, and here's what they'll say: *use colour.*

Ask brain researchers about a positive atmosphere conducive to thinking and learning, and here's what they'll propose: *a balanced-brain environment.*

As I said earlier, most of those who are making the rules in our world tend to be quite strong left-brain thinkers. That's very often what got them to their lofty positions in society in the first place. And their logical reasoning abilities are certainly to be admired, valued and respected. But, when left-brain attitudes completely overwhelm right-brain ideas, that lack of balance can prevent us from allowing our brains to achieve their natural and powerful potential.

It's been suggested by a number of experts that one of the keys to learning is emotion, and that the more senses we use, the better our brains will perform. They believe that the human brain is, in fact, by far the most sensual organ in our bodies.

What makes facts, ideas and events memorable and significant, then, is some kind of hook that arouses our souls in a way that stirs the senses. If the brain and the heart are to work together, we'd be wise to consider strengthening the dynamic role the right side of our brains can play in our lives.

BRAIN WAVES

08. Brain Power

With all the weaknesses in both our short-term and long-term memory systems, it's tempting to think that remembering things easily is truly an impossible task. Yet this is not at all the case.

Have you ever learned anything from a television infomercial? I actually learned an interesting little trick a few years ago by watching one that was selling a popular memory-training program.

In the commercial, the host asked those in a large studio audience to randomly call out words and names and numbers. (By the way, let's just assume that this exercise was legitimate and wasn't fraudulently set up ahead of time.)

After simply hearing a variety of people give him a list of 20 items, he then proceeded to repeat the items in exactly the same order that he'd heard them. The crowd was, quite naturally, very impressed with this gentleman's performance — and they were even more amazed later on when he repeated the list again, but backwards this time. Wouldn't you be too?

Given our predilection for forgetting just one name almost immediately after being introduced to someone, we're understandably impressed with a person who can remember twenty random, unrelated items in their correct sequence.

But the truth is that just about anyone can do this if given a basic understanding of how the human brain actually operates and what techniques can be used to exploit its power.

The following is a demonstration of what I mean. For this exercise, you'll need someone to read a list of unrelated words to you. Ask him or her to go through the list from top to bottom — once slowly (about one word every four seconds) and then one more time a little bit faster (about one word every two seconds). Your job is simply to listen to the list, try to remember as many of the words as you can, and then write them down on the following page.

Here's the list:

truck
cat
lawnmower
moon
chain
skyscraper
hat
tree
stove
apples
table
rake
mirror
football
bracelet
helicopter
door
bathtub
bridge
ghost

Write the words you remember here:

01.	11.
02.	12.
03.	13.
04.	14.
05.	15.
06.	16.
07.	17.
08.	18.
09.	19.
10.	20.

So how'd you do? Over the years, I've given memory tests like this to thousands of people from all walks of life, and individual results are incredibly consistent. If you're like most people who have taken this kind of test, you probably remembered between five and nine words. (That's the magic number seven again, plus or minus two.)

If you remembered more than nine words, you have a better-than-average ability to recall information — or perhaps a more natural inclination for learning — than most. Your performance, though, probably has very little to do with who you are.

Most people, from young children to senior citizens, achieve similar scores. Whatever your age, occupation, IQ, size of brain, level of education or gender, five to nine out of 20 is a typical result. (By the way, if you remembered just a handful of words from the beginning of the list and a few more words at the end, you're quite average indeed, as it's very common for people to remember the first and last items on a list.)

So here's the bad news: This is how most of us use our brains. It's the way, in fact, that we've been *trained* to use our brains — at an efficiency level of between 25 and 45%.

And, when you achieve this kind of result on a test like the one you've just done, you probably don't react with shock or surprise, because most of us believe that our memories simply don't work very well. We think having poor memories is a common human trait. If we believed otherwise, we wouldn't be terribly impressed by commercials on television that showcase others who appear to have excellent memories!

The reason most people perform poorly on memory tests like this, though, is likely that they've never learned how to use their brains the way they actually work best. However, you'll be happy to know that psychologists insist that human beings are born with essentially perfect memory systems.

And, to prove this point, I'd like you to try the exercise again, this time with a similar but different list of unrelated words. As before, have someone read the following to you twice, but ask them to read it exactly as it's written, emphasizing the capitalized, bold-faced words.

And, this time, I'll add two simple suggestions to the directions:

1. Don't try too hard. Stress and tension are major blocks to memory.
2. Don't think about the words themselves at all. Instead, just picture the items in your mind's eye. (You can use the huge screen inside your head, if you like.)

Here's the new list:

First, create a picture of a **CAR** *in your mind's eye — your car, a friend's car, a car you'd love to own.*

Now you see a **DOG** *in the driver's seat. Visualize a dog driving the car.*

On closer inspection, you notice that the dog is holding a large **BALLOON** *on a string. It's a big, red balloon.*

Watch the balloon break free and rise high in the air, so high that it travels directly toward the **SUN** *in the sky. Look directly at the big, yellow sun.*

Notice that there's a **ROPE** *tied around the sun — a strong, thick rope.*

Follow that rope back down toward the ground, where you see that the other end is attached to a **HOUSE.** *Your house, if you like. Or anybody's house.*

Here's a surprise: There's a gigantic **COWBOY HAT** *sitting on top of the house. It's the biggest cowboy hat you've ever seen.*

Growing right out the top of the cowboy hat is a bunch of **FLOWERS**. Have a good look at these beautiful, brightly coloured flowers.

Grab the flowers in one hand and place them on top of a **REFRIGERATOR**. They look pretty up there, don't they?

Now, open the door of the refrigerator and you'll see that it's filled with **ORANGES** — nothing but ripe, juicy oranges.

Of course, as soon as you open the door, those oranges come spilling out — and they pour onto and all around a **CHAIR**.

Leaning against the chair is a **SHOVEL** — a regular, garden-variety shovel.

Pick up the shovel, swing it hard, and use it to smash a **WINDOW**. Hit the window hard, breaking the glass, and jump through to the other side.

When you land on the ground outside, you see a **BASKETBALL** on the ground. Pick up the basketball.

Oddly enough, there's a **WATCH** strapped around the basketball. It's a really big watch!

On the face of the watch is a picture of an **AIRPLANE**. Have a good look at this airplane.

Suddenly, the airplane lifts right off the watchface and starts to fly away. Uh-oh. It flies smack into a **STOP SIGN**. See the plane hit the stop sign hard, knocking it off and into the air.

Look at the stop sign flying through the air, and see it drop with a splash into a **SWIMMING POOL**.

Dive into the pool. Underneath the water — at the far end of the pool — you swim up to a mysterious-looking **DOOR**.

Open the door slowly. Behind the door is an **ALIEN** *standing there, grinning at you. You faint.*

OK, here's the list one more time. This time, have it repeated to you a bit faster:

See a **CAR** *and, sitting in the driver's seat, there's a* **DOG**.

Notice that the dog is holding a **BALLOON** *which rises up toward the* **SUN**.

Wrapped around the sun is a **ROPE** *which is connected, at the other end, to a* **HOUSE**.

On top of the house is a **COWBOY HAT** *with a bunch of* **FLOWERS** *growing out of the top.*

Take that bunch of flowers and place them on top of the **REFRIGERATOR**, *which is filled with* **ORANGES** — *so full that they're pouring out.*

As the oranges tumble out and land on and all around a **CHAIR**, *notice a* **SHOVEL** *leaning against it.*

Grab the shovel and smash the **WINDOW**, *jumping through to pick up a* **BASKETBALL**.

There's a big **WATCH** strapped around the basketball, and on the face of the watch is a picture of an **AIRPLANE**.

The airplane takes off and smashes into a **STOP SIGN** which flies through the air and lands in a **SWIMMING POOL**.

Dive in! Open the underwater **DOOR** at the end of the pool and look into the eyes of the smiling **ALIEN**.

Now, let's see if you can write down that list of words in the correct order. (Don't get flustered if you can't remember one of the words. If that happens, simply try going to the end of the list and work backwards instead.)

01.	11.
02.	12.
03.	13.
04.	14.
05.	15.
06.	16.
07.	17.
08.	18.
09.	19.
10.	20.

If you're like most of the individuals to whom I've given similar tests, you probably achieved results significantly better than your performance on the first test of your memory. It's very likely that the number of words filled in for the second memory test far exceeds the number of words filled in for the first one. In fact, many people surprise themselves and remember all the words in exactly the right sequence — and can even repeat them in reverse order as well.

The good news, then, is that your memory can work quite successfully after all. (The bad news is that, when you store these words using the proper techniques as has just been demonstrated, you'll not only remember the words now, but you'll remember them days and weeks and maybe even months later. I've had people, long after they've done this exercise, ask me to get the list out of their heads because it was apparently driving them crazy!)

Now, of course, being able to repeat a simple list of words isn't especially important or useful. On its own, it's little more than a parlour trick. Its significance, though, lies in the fact that it proves this point:

> *Human beings are quite capable of using their memory systems at superior levels of efficiency.*

While your performance on the first memory test is a good example of how most people unfortunately use their brains, it's important that we understand how and why the 'trick' used for the second test works and then apply this knowledge to the real memory and learning situations we face in our day-to-day lives.

It's really too bad that, because of the way most of us have been trained to use our brains — or, more to the point, how *not* to use our brains — we labour under the misconception that we're incapable of performing well on a variety of simple mental challenges. However, your performance on the second test is an elementary example of the true capabilities of your natural memory system.

The purpose of such a memory trick at this point is to illustrate the difference between what we think our brains can do and what they're actually capable of doing. Remembering the second list of words is really much more, though, than just a trick; it is, in fact, the result of using our brains the way they truly work. And it's not just about putting pictures in our heads, as you might be thinking.

Interestingly, being able to perform a mental feat such as remembering a list of 20 unrelated words gives the impression of what's generally regarded as intelligence. The truth is, however, that most of us are quite capable of mastering this kind of achievement.

When my daughter, Jane, was seven years old, I decided to do a little family research and explore the possibility of plumbing the depths of her brain power. As the two of us traveled together down a highway in my car, I recited the previous list of 20 words to her — exactly as you've just had someone recite it to you.

And, lo and behold, she remembered all the words in the correct order, immediately after hearing them. She also remembered the list later that day, as well as the next day, and the following week, and even months later.

She was so proud of herself (as I was, too, of course) that we decided to try some more brain tricks. So I showed her how to memorize the calendar, mentally pinpointing the specific day of the week after being given a particular month and date.

After only a few minutes of instruction and a small amount of practice, she figured it out and could do the calendar trick just as well as I could. Hungry for more, she asked me about something else I'd demonstrated to her in the past. She wanted to know how I'd learned to recite the alphabet forward and backward at the same time (i.e. Z, A, Y, B, X, C, W...). So I explained the process to her, and she learned how to do it. And she remembers it to this day, many years later.

The next week, she went off to school with the Show & Tell of all Show & Tells, ready to knock the socks off her teacher and her classmates. And that she did. The teacher was so impressed that she suggested Jane be placed in the school's gifted program!

Activating brainpower to learn new information requires both the understanding and the conscious application of several principles and strategies. It demands a basic comprehension of how our brains operate, an insight into techniques that push our brains to work at peak efficiency, and an effort to combine the strengths of both sides of our brains.

Once we're clear on these concepts, we can then put the basics of brain training to use and pump up our mental performance. As we begin trusting and using these skills, we'll learn to cope better with the problems of information overload and fully exploit the potential of our minds.

Using our brains efficiently and potently requires the understanding and conscious application of seven simple principles. Let's call the following, then, the brain-training basics:

MOTIVATION

PRACTICE

ASSOCIATION

MEANING

VISUALIZATION

CHUNKING

EMOTION

Read on, my friends. Enlightenment awaits.

BRAIN WAVES

BRAIN-TRAINING BASICS

The elevator to success is out of order.
You'll have to use the stairs — one step at a time.

Joe Girard

09. Motivation

At one point in Episode V of the *Star Wars* movies, Yoda, that brainy old guru-goblin, became angry when his pupil, Luke Skywalker, kept complaining that the training he was doing and the lessons he was learning were really tough. In response, Luke told Yoda that he'd try harder when facing these new challenges.

Yoda's reaction to Luke's angst, of course, was classic brain-training advice: "Try not. Do or do not. There is no try."

Having shared that quote with you, I'm also here to tell you that, while I certainly admire the little guy's wisdom — he is, after all, one of the great sages in movie history — it's important to understand the following inescapable fact: There is no *do* without *try*.

All of us know people with sharp minds, and we admire them. We especially revere those around us who seem to have better memories than our own. You know who they are:

They remember names, telephone numbers and passwords after hearing them only once or twice.

They make presentations without so much as a glance at a scrap of text for guidance.

They hear directions once and then travel directly to their destination.

They speak at meetings, following a logical, obviously predetermined, order — again without having to refer to notes.

How on earth do these smarter-than-us folks do it, we wonder? Were they given an unfair advantage by being born with better brains than the rest of us? Have they been endowed with some kind of genetic boost that has supercharged their mindpower in some way? Are they somehow blessed with stronger memory systems than most mere mortals possess?

*The answer to these questions is a resounding **no**!*

Psychologists, don't forget, like to say that most human beings are born with pretty well perfect memory systems. When we popped out of the womb, we were remarkable little creatures who quite naturally used both sides of our brains, working together as a team, to learn and remember.

And learn and remember we did. In fact, we adults often refer to infants and toddlers as 'learning sponges'. We find it remarkable that young children are capable of learning amazing amounts of information so quickly and, apparently, with such ease.

Well, they're motivated to learn, aren't they? They have what appears to be a practically insatiable thirst for knowledge. They seek out new knowledge and, in their own way, they work hard at learning and remembering.

As we age, though, we unfortunately develop the impression that, slowly but surely, we will naturally lose this ability to use our brains quite so efficiently. We seem to assume that, no matter what we do, we're inescapably bound to get older and dumber. But that's where we're wrong.

Let's compare what we know about how humans learn to the way some attend to their physical health. Scientists, doctors, nutritionists and kinesiologists have made great learning strides over the years. Their studies tell us just about everything we need to know about how to get our bodies into shape and how to keep them operating at peak efficiency.

Many people, though, don't heed the message. They disregard their physical health, but not because of inadequate research or lack of understanding. Rather, they neglect their bodies because they're too un-motivated to do what's necessary to get into shape and continue to do the maintenance.

They don't find time to exercise, they stuff their faces with junk food, and they ignore their need for adequate sleep. They know what needs to be done, but they can't be bothered to do it. They don't try.

Well, the same applies to the way we treat learning, in spite of the tremendous gains we've made in our understanding of the way our brains operate and of the things that need to be done to keep them functioning at peak performance. And the main reason is this:

We simply don't make the effort.

For example, surveys over the years have suggested that over 80% of adults claim their number one memory problem is remembering names, an event that occurs over and over again in both our personal and working lives. In fact, we're often very embarrassed at our seeming inability to recall a name introduced mere seconds prior to an introductory handshake.

To cover up this inadequacy, we often resort to various subversive techniques, such as saying: "Hello... (pause)... How are you?" or "Hi... (pause)... Nice to meet you!" And, after that initial embarrassment, we suffer through hours, days, months, even years of hiding the fact that we're apparently too feeble-minded to learn simple names.

(Given that this is such a common problem — and since it's unlikely we'll ever live in a world where we'll all wear permanent name tags — maybe we should just get over this original bewilderment and simply say: "I'm sorry. What was your name again?" This would at least give us another shot at remembering the name. And you know what? The other person will be *so grateful* to hear your name one more time as well.)

But we continue to fumble along with the name game. Rather than do something about it, we simply wish we were smart like those few showoffs we know who are introduced to someone new, shake hands, repeat the name and somehow store it permanently in their long-term memories. Oh, if only we were brainy like that too!

Well, we are. Really, we are. In fact, the only significant difference between the name-rememberers and the name-forgetters is that one group tries and the other one doesn't. The name-rememberers make a serious and sincere effort to remember:

- They mentally prepare ahead of time.
- They focus their full attention on the introduction.
- They keep repeating the name after it's been stored.

The name-forgetters (more than four out of five people) do none of these things. They rarely give the introduction a moment's thought ahead of time, and they think about all kinds of unrelated issues at the moment of introduction. (How do I look? How important is this person to me? How much should I say? Do I want to know this person better? Is my handshake firm enough?) Then they quickly move on to other thoughts as soon as the introduction has been made. And they wonder why they don't remember the person's name later!

Effort, folks. *Motivation.* And, of course, this simple concept of trying harder has a multitude of implications with regard to issues much more important to our lives than simply trying to remember someone's name when introduced.

Think about the last time you sat down at the beginning of a meeting, a presentation or a lecture. Did you make a conscious effort in any way to remember what was about to be said? Did you use any specific techniques to focus your attention while someone else was speaking? Did you use follow-up strategies at the end of the session that would facilitate recall later?

Perhaps not. And that's a problem. Because, when we're engaged in passive learning experiences like reading and listening (as we so often are), this lack of effort and motivation can have dire consequences that very much affect the way we use our brains.

READING

The principle of motivation applies big time to a very common passive learning experience — reading.

Reading is a skill we teach, but just until young people can read at a pretty basic level. And then, inexplicably, reading instruction quite suddenly stops. After that, very little attention is paid to how its passive nature so often impedes learning and wastes time. In fact, once children advance from oral to silent reading, they tend to be left pretty well on their own.

It's as if we believe that reading passively is all there is to it.

It's one thing to read works of literature passively, by the way, as such material tends to lend itself to imagination and emotional reaction. However, reading expository, or informational, material — as we most often do in school and certainly at work — is quite a different story.

Here's how the problem is initially established: To reduce the financial burden on families of school-aged children, school boards lend textbooks to students with the admonition that they're not supposed to write in the books or mark them up in any way.

Lamentably, they're trained to read with their eyes (passively) and not with their pens (actively) — and, as an unfortunate result of this practice, not with their brains either.

Motivation is essential to reading. It's extremely difficult to comprehend informational material by simply moving our eyeballs and turning pages. To read, understand and recall the information later, it's imperative that we're as actively engaged in the process as possible. This applies to everything we read — in school, at work and in our personal lives.

Our schools don't always help us engage in this process of active reading. In fact, they very often (unintentionally, of course) encourage the opposite. If students aren't allowed to write directly in their textbooks, then shouldn't we be teaching them instead to make useful notes while they read the material?

If this practice is taking place at all, it's being done poorly, because the vast majority of high school graduates I've spoken to tell me they've never been shown how to properly take notes and, in fact, don't really know the first place to start.

When they continue their education or enter the workforce, our high school graduates intuitively seize the opportunity to read and learn more actively. And how do they do that? They start using highlighters. But what's the #1 mistake they make in this, their first excursion into the world of active reading?

THEY HIGHLIGHT <u>EVERYTHING</u>.

They highlight the first sentence of the paragraph, as they probably should do, because it incorporates the main idea about 70% of the time. Then they underline the second sentence because it seems pretty important, too. Then the third sentence. And the last, which includes the main idea about 20% of the time, as well.

In other words, they primarily transform white pages with black printing into yellow (or pink or green) pages with black printing! And, in doing so, they actually sabotage an opportunity for active learning by turning it into an ineffective learning experience that rolls along on automatic pilot.

In fact, the whole point of highlighting is to engage in an active experience that involves motivation. But, if the process involves little more than indiscriminately drawing attention to every single line, regardless of the importance of its content, then that effort is wasted because of the mindlessness of the method.

What's required, if we're to even begin experiencing some consistently successful thinking and learning experiences, is some kind of deliberate effort. Without effort, in fact, the other brain-training basics just won't work.

Truly, one of the fallacies of the kinds of self-help programs so very often advertised on television infomercials is that they're offered as effortless learning experiences. If we just send in our money, read the manuals, watch the videos and/or listen to the sound clips, we'll suddenly be transformed — apparently without even trying!

Life, of course, generally isn't quite that easy. Just as a student's method of sitting in bed reading notes over and over again doesn't work (because it's too easy and doesn't require much effort), so being a passive receptor of commercially produced learning programs won't be successful either.

We live in a society that wants desperately to believe in the quick fix, some kind of easy and effortless magic potion:

Take a one-day course and be more assertive right away!

Attend a weekend retreat and solve all your relationship problems!

Listen to a CD and learn a new language in just three weeks!

We can now shop at a local drugstore, supermarket or health food store and buy smart pills. Just pop a few of these tablets in your mouth and — *presto* — you're instantly the smartest person in town. Well, I hate to burst any bubbles here, but you know what? That's just not going to happen.

LISTENING

A few years ago, I was invited to speak to the teachers of a large, urban high school.

I couldn't help but notice before beginning my presentation to them that, of the 100 or so participants in attendance, the large majority of them were going to listen to me without the use of pen and paper. It seemed obvious to me, even before I started speaking, that only a very small number in my audience were prepared to make enough of an effort to truly attend to what I was going to say.

And so I wondered how much learning was actually going to take place with my audience that day. I thought: If educators themselves haven't been trained properly to learn and remember, then what hope does everyone else have?

If those who are entrusted with the education of our young people aren't themselves acutely aware of the limitations of passive learning, then how can we possibly expect that their students will engage in successful classroom learning experiences?

And, if students don't 'learn how to learn' while they're in school, then what does that say about the future of the workplace learning and training that will inevitably follow after graduation?

By the way, my intention here is certainly not to place all the blame for our learning faults on educators alone. Not at all. It seems that the same lack of effort to learn occurs at workplace events as well — at meetings, seminars, workshops and conferences. And it's not just the participants themselves who are at fault. It's often the speakers too.

As a participant, a listener, attending a great many presentations myself, I'm often amazed at the lack of effort exhibited by many speakers at engaging the attention of their audiences. Surely, the responsibility for learning must be shared by all who are involved in the process.

While learning theories and memory techniques abound, we won't be able to learn better unless we actually practice the strategies. Even if certain vitamins and nutrients can, in fact, create changes in our bodies and in our minds, we won't make our brains work better unless we consciously use them properly.

Effort, my friends. **Motivation**.

And, once we accept the fact that we must first try harder to learn, we can then make a commitment to taking good old Yoda's prudent advice. Once we invoke the effort, then — and only then — will we be able to take a legitimate shot at *doing*.

BRAIN WAVES

10. Practice

Practice is the most commonly used strategy we use to learn and remember. What's another word for practice? Rehearsal. And how do we rehearse? By repeating the same thing over and over again.

Practice works. If it didn't, it wouldn't be included here as a brain-training basic. There's no denying that repetition strengthens the recall trace of concepts being committed to memory. From the moment of birth, we use it to transfer information from our short-term to our long-term memory systems.

Constant repetition of words like 'mama' and 'dada' worked these words into our baby brains after a relatively short period of time, until we were saying them and understanding what they meant. We learned 'dog' and 'TV' and 'car' through the same process; this is, in fact, how we first developed our vocabularies. After hearing often enough that a 'door' is that large slab of hard material with the shiny knob on it, we soon came to recognize its name.

Practice is a learning technique drummed into our heads as children in school where we were encouraged to memorize facts, formulas, spelling tricks, grammar rules, foreign words, definitions, poetry and the multiplication tables.

After hearing, saying and copying out the seven times table ad infinitum, we eventually know with a considerable degree of certainty that $7 \times 8 = 56$, and we remember this fact for the rest of our lives with no difficulty at all.

In high schools, colleges and universities, students continue to place their ultimate faith in practice as a learning technique. They read their notes over and over and, given some extra time, read them again.

They study together in groups and repeat material unremittingly until it sinks in. In fact, it's quite possible that the act of writing an examination is a concept originally conceived by educators to encourage and promote practice as an appropriate method of learning.

Quite naturally, we later take this popular strategy into the workplace with us: reading and rereading reports, practicing speeches and presentations, listening to instructions more than once and repeating them aloud so we can remember them later. Instructors, trainers, supervisors and co-workers consistently help to enshrine the act of repetition as the primary tool for learning. It worked for our grandparents. It worked for our parents. So...

As I say, practice works. But this, the second basic of brain training, has a couple of flaws — and major ones at that. Certainly, it doesn't deserve its popularity as the most embraced technique used by so many of us to learn information. As a matter of fact, it should really be considered the weakest of the seven principles.

And here's why: The problem is that saying aloud, hearing, or writing the same thing over and over and over again leads to two very significant brain-busting problems:

IT'S BORING.

IT'S TIME-CONSUMING.

As has been explained previously, boring information practically shuts our brains down. Brains are simply not at all prepared to allow tedious information in. Words and numbers that are constantly repeated ad nauseum are offensive to the brain, and so it will do all it can to send them away each and every time they come calling.

The more uninteresting the material, the more unlikely it is that our brains will consider that information worthy of transfer into our long-term memory systems. As a result, most things we try to learn through simple practice will skip in and pop out of short-term memory in a matter of seconds.

So the boredom factor can seriously negate practice as a viable learning strategy. The second problem is the time it takes to commit facts and ideas to memory using the rehearsal technique.

But, you say, practice worked just fine with the seven times table, thank you very much. And you're right; it did. But did we learn the seven times table by spending just a couple of hours repeating it? Or maybe nine or ten hours?

No, we didn't. We repeated the seven times table many more times than that — hour after hour, day after day, week after week, month after month, year after year. And sure enough, as adults, we now know for a fact that $7 \times 8 = 56$.

To be sure, schoolchildren might have some things going on in their lives that interfere with their ability to study. But, let's face it, eight-year-olds still have plenty of time for practice as their primary learning strategy. As adults, though, we sure don't.

In the workplace, this problem has intensified considerably. Most of us find it difficult enough to find time to read e-mail messages, memos, letters, reports and newsletters even once, let alone several times.

So we need to put practice in its rightful place. Let's include it on the list of brain-training basics but knock it off its pedestal of supreme importance, all right?

It's useful for young people to repeat BEDMAS as a way to recall the order of operations in math because it's simple and it doesn't eat up a lot of time. But trying to easily remember *brackets, exponents, division, multiplication, addition and subtraction* without that first-letter trick? I don't think so. Why not? It's too boring. It's too time-consuming. It's too brain-busting.

So it's helpful to commit to memory the essential points of a presentation we must make, preferably with the help of a trick (like a mnemonic device), but not nearly such a good idea to attempt its complete memorization.

And it's appropriate to read over a synopsis of a report a few times (or, even better, a synopsis of the synopsis), but ludicrous to tackle serial rereading of the complete report.

Practice does belong on the brain-training list, for sure. But other strategies, in combination with the act of simple repetition, can very much help make up for its limitations and even enhance its effectiveness. So we need to add some more principles to help negotiate our way through the learning maze.

BRAIN WAVES

11. Association

The principle of association, the act of relating individual elements to each other, is at the core of most memory training programs. For example, when we're introduced to someone new, we're told that the best way to remember the name is to associate it to a physical characteristic of that person.

So, when I'm about to be introduced, I must consciously make an effort to form a connection between, for instance, that person's name and face. If the individual's name is Tom and his face reminds me of a turtle, then I'll think of him as Tommy The Turtle.

Two weeks later, when I see him walking towards me again, I'll note his turtle-like features, give him a big wave and call out: "Hi, Tom. How's it going?" This makes me look like a smart guy because Tom, if he's like most human beings, has by this time forgotten my name altogether.

So here's the rule:

In order to learn and remember new information,
we must associate it with something easy to remember.

The human mind, oddly enough, remembers two things stuck together better than it does single items. That infomercial hosts can repeat complete lists of items heard only once is, to most people, surprising enough. That they're able to recall the information in the correct order (both forwards and backwards) seems almost miraculous!

The truth is, though, that learning material out of order would be quite a bit more difficult. In fact, the infomercial hucksters probably wouldn't be able to do it. It's the principle of association that makes this exercise quite within the bounds of most people's capabilities.

When words on a memory test are given (or, more to the point, are processed) in pairs rather than as single items, one word acts as a clue to the next word, and that word is a link to the next one, etc. A few chapters back, the *car* reminded you of the *dog*, the dog of the *balloon*, the balloon of the *sun*. By the same means, in reverse order, the *alien* made you think of the *door*, the door of the *swimming pool*, and the swimming pool of the *stop sign*. Without using an associative technique, most of us would find this exercise next to impossible.

The principle of association, then, must be applied if we're to quickly and easily learn new information. It's certainly evident that it applies to remembering names and word lists, as illustrated in the previous examples. But it's also significant in many other learning situations as well — not only when we must simply remember material ourselves, but when we want to communicate information memorably to others.

Let's first agree on the premise that, if we deem to speak about something to someone else, it's desirable that they pay attention to what we have to say. Likewise, if we choose to write to others, it's again our wish that they both understand and remember our words, and the meaning of those words, at a later date. If this weren't the case, why would we bother speaking or writing at all in the first place?

This is where the principle of association has a critical application. When we communicate with others, whether it be in oral or written form, we'd be wise to consciously associate new information with something else that our audience already knows. Preferably, that something should be interesting (or even strange).

What's called The Rule Of Ridiculous Association suggests that the more bizarre the connection, the more likely we'll remember the information. Tommy The Turtle works better than Tommy The Guy With The Moustache because imagining a human being as a turtle is much more interesting and unusual than simply thinking of someone with hair on his lip. As a result, we should make an effort to create uncommon connections when we communicate with others, particularly when the information is so dry, bland and routine that it probably won't be, on its own, unique enough to be memorable.

How do we put this into practice? By finding provocative examples to illustrate mundane ideas, that's how. By choosing language that attracts attention rather than employing the same words that everyone else would use. By avoiding clichés because, after a hundred people tell you to "have a nice day", the phrase is rendered impotent by its overuse.

Another example: If, out of 50 résumés submitted as job applications, all but one close with the phrase "References available upon request", isn't it likely that the one concluding with an even slightly different phrase will receive at least a bit more attention? The more pedestrian the material we're working with, then, the more we should consider using associative techniques.

For instance, music instructors have historically understood that few of their students would find it easy to remember that the notes on the treble clef scale are E-G-B-D-F. There's certainly nothing significant or memorable about these five sequential letters on their own. On the other hand, presenting a meaningful series of words such as *Every Good Boy Deserves Fudge* or *Eat Good Bread Dear Father* or *Elephants Got Big Dirty Feet* has worked remarkably well for millions upon millions of people on this planet — very few of whom have ever actually needed to recall these notes!

Using mnemonic devices in this way, making mundane information memorable as well as more quickly and easily learnable by attaching it to something else which is significantly more profound, is a good example of a practical way to put the principle of association into practice.

When we train others to communicate, both in school and in the workplace, this is something that needs to be emphasized. I must admit, though, that I myself have been confronted with some opposition to the concept that making memorable associations when we speak and write is truly a worthwhile idea. I've been told, for instance, that "that's not the way I was taught to make presentations when I was in school" and "that's not the way people write in my office". Here's my response to these kinds of skeptical reactions:

"How many people, do you think, remember your words even an hour after you speak?" and *"How truly effective are your workplace reading and writing experiences, given the fact that the majority of the material is presented in exactly the same way?"*

The principle of association is a useful one. Many experts in the fields of neuroscience and memory research consider it an essential tool that dispatches information forcefully into our long-term memory systems, so we really should take advantage of its power.

Are the puzzle pieces now beginning to fit together?

BRAIN WAVES

12. Meaning

When things make sense to us, we tend to understand them — and, when we understand, we're better able to remember.

Learning meaningful material is much easier than trying to learn incomprehensible information, to be sure. For example, try to memorize the following series of 12 nonsense words:

ase ot tou nad rhrabou het fo otu tengyl pisls toba eth

Having some trouble? I imagine you are. Such a series of meaningless combinations of letters is neither understandable nor memorable because you have nothing logical to relate them to. The 'words' don't make sense, so it's more or less like trying to decipher a foreign language.

Now try this:

gently sea to out and slips harbour of out boat the the

While this series might be a bit difficult to learn quickly, you can certainly memorize it better than the previous one — because you're already familiar with the words being used.

They're in a nonsensical order, but each word on its own has meaning, so you're likely to be successful remembering these words more easily and in a shorter period of time than the 'words' in the previous series.

How about this next one?

The boat slips gently out of the harbour and out to sea

Quite likely, you could remember this 12-word series after only one or two readings. Not only do the words make sense, but they're presented this time in a logical, sequential and sensible order. Meaning greatly facilitates learning and memory.

This principle makes sense but is often ignored when it comes to dealing with day-to-day tasks. We constantly waste effort and time trying to learn and remember material that's presented to us by others.

People don't, of course, normally communicate as badly as I've suggested with the first list of nonsense words on the previous page. They often do so, though, in a different way than we ourselves would present the same information. But, instead of restructuring the words and ideas of others, we accept them exactly as they're given and try to learn them in a way that makes sense... to someone else.

This method of learning is, according to the principle of meaning, quite illogical. Attending to this principle means taking information as it's given and instantly changing it so it makes more sense to us and the way we ourselves think and learn.

This means that young people shouldn't just be told to 'study' what textbook authors and teachers write and say. They should, instead, be encouraged to take the information that's offered and translate it into a structure, an organization and a style of language that makes sense to them.

Successful learners are aware of this principle, as are effective educators and trainers. But they follow this maxim more as a result of intuition than because of the kind of specific training that all of us, rightfully, should have been given in the first place.

The principle of meaning is certainly understood by those who are successful in public life and business and industry. With the kinds of demands we're up against today, reaching the pinnacle of our professions will undoubtedly not happen unless we learn to understand and remember new information quickly. Sadly, most of us have never been trained to do this properly, labouring under the burden imposed by slow and inefficient learning methods.

Reading a document, even many times over, simply won't stick information into our long-term memory systems, at least not without much more rehearsal time than any of us can possibly find time for in these days of data inundation.

For instance, the most efficient way to read a report once and be able to recollect its contents later is to read it in chunks, from one heading to the next, and briefly summarize what we read, either in the report's margins or on a separate piece of paper.

Using our own words — that mean something to us personally — to précis the report's information in such chunks forces us to engage in three brain-enriching activities: (1) we're forced to think about what we're reading in order to write; (2) the act of writing is an active learning process; and (3) restructuring someone else's words and translating them so they make sense to us helps us understand the material better.

When we've finished our reading, having used this technique, we'll be in the advantageous position of not only having a greater understanding of the material than usual, but also of having a condensed version (in our own words) that we can review quickly and easily at a later date, the time normally reserved for ponderous rehearsal strategies having automatically been reduced substantially.

Please note that I'm deliberately recommending notetaking over highlighting as a chosen learning method. When we highlight, we simply take note of the author's main points — or, at least, those concepts we deem most important to us. This process has limited use unless we take it one step further and actively rewrite those ideas in words of our own.

It's the rewriting, after all, that compels us to understand someone else's ideas in ways that have meaning to us. The mere act of highlighting on its own just doesn't make us think hard enough about what we're reading, and so it isn't nearly as useful.

Most of us have a habit of reading with minimal understanding for a couple of reasons:

We were never properly trained to actively read for meaning.

Reading efficiently requires more effort than we're willing to expend.

Because of this, we devote considerably more time than is necessary to the simple act of reading — and then rapidly forget what we read. Again, I've been just as guilty as anyone else when it comes to having squandered time and energy by using inefficient and unproductive learning strategies.

Believe me, there have been plenty of instances in the past when I've spent way too much time trying to memorize material that I didn't actually understand in the first place. I often wasn't devoting my full attention, I didn't always adequately comprehend the concepts as they were presented to me, and I rarely asked questions (the easiest and fastest way to learn) because I was afraid of looking foolish in front of my peers.

And so I dedicated far too many hours of my precious time to the practically useless, not to mention mind-numbing, process of repetition in an effort to learn the information.

WHAT A WASTE OF TIME!

BRAIN WAVES

13. Visualization

A picture is worth a thousand words. That sure is a catchy phrase, isn't it? Well, actually, it's a lot more than just memorable:

IT'S TRUE! IT'S TRUE! IT'S TRUE!

Why do more than 80% of adults forget names and only half that number have trouble remembering faces? Why are people's faces, in other words, more than twice as easy to recollect as their names?

Well, it's because faces are visual. And visual characteristics make a powerful imprint on our brains quite naturally, while words require a much more concentrated effort before being cemented, with any degree of success, into our long-term memory systems.

The principle of visualization has far-reaching implications on learning. We live in a culture that utterly worships the printed word. Our educational institutions and our workplaces are packed to the rafters with words, words, words.

Even if we do eventually arrive at the day when we will live in a totally paperless society (although that doesn't seem likely any time soon), the words aren't suddenly going to disappear. We'll just see them on screens or even suspended in the air instead of on pieces of paper, that's all. And so we'll continue to be expected to learn many things via the printed word.

This is a BIG problem. But it's not so huge an issue that we can't considerably lessen its implications.

While it's quite clear that we can't always turn all our words into big, colourful cartoon pictures, we can at least work harder to present written information in a more visually appealing form. In spite of the fact that we've moved into a world of communications that provides a plethora of presentation choices, we've been obstinately slow when it comes to taking advantage of these many new options.

The format of much written material generated today in our schools and workplaces mirrors material produced 20 years ago. In spite of living in a computer age, with its myriad of options, we continue to present information in pretty well the same old way we did before the advent of these technological breakthroughs.

Certainly there are particular formats that many of us are encouraged to comply with when, for instance, writing e-mail messages, memos and business letters. Many organizations, for totally appropriate reasons, insist that both internal and outgoing reports follow specific guidelines. That's understandable for a variety of reasons, such as clarity, coherence and consistency.

Books (like this one) normally adhere to a basic set of guidelines that encourage product conformity at an affordable cost. But, especially when producing multimedia presentations, informal documents or personal material, we don't have to so blindly accommodate the status quo, the tried and true, any more.

Today, with so many choices — such a dramatic variety of fonts, print sizes, graphics and colours — we often have the opportunity to add lots of extra life to our work. Surely we should be reveling in the variety of options now available to us.

We can now enter into this new world of technological innovation that has the capability of generating material that's so much more stimulating. There is such a choice of features we can embrace to make important things stand out! We can...

increase the size of the text.

change the font once in a while.

boldface some of the material.

italicize letters and numbers.

outline them.

condense words .

s t r e t c h   t h e m   o u t.

add shapes.

use ⟶ arrows.

insert graphics: ☺ .

use • • • bullets.

even use ☼☼☼ fancy bullets.

WE HAVE THE CAPABILITY!

The advertising industry, of course, is well aware of the power of visual presentation. It's no coincidence that television commercials, online advertising and print ads in media such as newspapers and magazines often lean much more heavily on imagery than on written content.

Even radio advertising is mindful of appealing to the senses. Lacking the obvious opportunity to present information visually, it uses other nonverbal tricks by emphasizing voice tone, inflection and volume. In fact, advertising professionals are the most powerful brain trainers of our time, given that their livelihoods depend on hammering information into our brains.

We should, then, put into practice what advertisers already know about using the principle of visualization to influence our memory systems. Both in learning situations and when we simply want to communicate with others, we should make a strong effort to attend to the power of visual appeal.

When we're the receivers rather than the senders of information, too, we'd be wise to restructure the material so that its newly formed imagery creates a much improved opportunity to have a compelling impact on what goes on inside our brains.

BRAIN WAVES

14. Chunking

Breaking down information into chunks gives the brain some breathing space. Chunks (groups, sections, blocks, pieces) create breaks that allow our brains to deal with information one bit at a time rather than in one large, incomprehensible mass.

The principle of chunking underlies the way much information is presented — from the way meetings are broken down into distinct agenda items, to the format of speeches and presentations, to the layout of résumés, to the practice of using verses in poetry, to the separation of prose into paragraphs. Trying to listen to or read thousands of words as one singular, huge informational block often proves to be intimidating and too difficult for us.

Those responsible for creating a format for the written English language, long before brain research had determined the reasons why, somehow understood intuitively that paragraphs were a necessary function of efficient writing and reading.

Today, the modern inclination to use a full-block correspondence style, with both margins justified and, perhaps, double-spacing between paragraphs, is one good example of the evolution of writing towards a more visually appealing and chunked presentation style.

Communication experts suggest, too, that most business documents should incorporate only three- or four-sentence paragraphs and should probably take up no more than six to ten typed lines of print.

But simply dividing our written sentences into paragraphs is only a beginning. There are many more ways that we can make written material more appealing to a reader's brain. The example a few pages back of adding visual impact to written material, for example, is an illustration of how chunking can improve both communication and the learning process.

To enhance information and make it more powerful, we should consider avoiding the overly consistent use of the standard paragraph form. Whenever we're in a position where we're trying to communicate a number of points that we want to make particularly memorable, we should present that material, for example, in bulleted lists.

Another way to emphasize pertinent chunks is to highlight certain points by creating a simple visual shape, or frame, around the material in question. These organizational methods immediately provide our brains with a better chance of focusing attention on the information and being able to recall it later.

Because many readers, due either to strict time constraints or to insufficient motivation, merely skim written material, it's important that we invest some effort to make the most noteworthy points easy for people to notice. We want these details to...

 JUMP OFF THE PAGE!

And that's where chunking comes in. This principle, like all the other basics previously mentioned, applies both to communicating with others and to learning information ourselves.

One of the biggest problems we face both as readers, listeners and learners is that we become easily overwhelmed. And, when we feel swamped, what begins as overload can quickly lead to brain shutdown.

Taking material we must attend to and breaking it down into chunks is a potent way to avoid this kind of breakdown. For example, let's say you're given ten minutes to read the following material and remember its main points later:

It's important that we understand the importance of brain training and the remarkable impact it can have on our lives, both personally and professionally. Brain training actually influences literally everything we do. Using its principles can help us develop recall tricks that can be used in innumerable situations. It can enhance the way we write messages, letters, memos and reports — particularly with respect to different formats that attract attention.

Training our brains properly can lead to strategies necessary to improved notetaking, a skill few of us ever learned very well when we were in school. We can discover new techniques to refine the way we advertise and market products and services. Our oral presentations can change in style so that what we say makes a powerful impression on those who hear us. And our own listening skills can be cultivated, too, with an understanding of how our brains function best.

Now, based on the concepts discussed so far, what would you say would be the most inefficient method of learning this information? Spending the ten minutes reading it over and over and over, right? Understanding the principle of chunking should encourage us instead to go through it once, decide what are its salient points, and then jot down what they are, like so:

THE USES OF BRAIN TRAINING

1. Develops recall tricks

2. Enhances writing formats

3. Improves notetaking strategies

4. Refines advertising and marketing

5. Formulates new styles of oral presentations

6. Cultivates listening skills

Now, that wasn't so hard, was it? A little bit of effort, a pinch of thought and a touch of active learning, et voilà — progress. Psychologically, a list of the six main uses of brain training seems much easier to digest and remember. Even if we've now used half of our ten minutes, we're already ahead of the game.

But just breaking it down from a paragraph to a group of phrases isn't enough. The chunking isn't done yet. Why not continue the process and break the information down some more, this time by picking out out key words in each of the phrases?

THE USES OF BRAIN TRAINING

1. Develops *recall* tricks

2. Enhances *writing* formats

3. Improves *notetaking* strategies

4. Refines *advertising* and marketing

5. Formulates new styles of *oral presentations*

6. Cultivates *listening* skills

Now we're getting somewhere! It makes sense, after all, that learning a list of six words will be easier than memorizing a list of six phrases, just as remembering a list of six phrases was easier than learning a whole paragraph.

But we're not finished yet. If we can go from paragraphs to phrases and phrases to words, then we might as well continue the chunking process and break the information down even further, this time from words to letters: RWNAOL.

But RWNAOL doesn't actually make any sense, and so it will be difficult to learn. We'll now have to somehow turn this meaningless collection of letters into something more memorable. If the order of the six main points isn't important, we can scramble the letters to form something more recognizable, such as RAN LOW:

R *(recall)*   **L** *(listening)*

A *(advertising)*   **O** *(oral presentations)*

N *(notetaking)*   **W** *(writing)*

Or, if the order of the listed items is important, then we can create a simple mnemonic device using the first letters of each word to form a memorable sentence: **R**eally **W**hat's **N**ecessary **A**re **O**ptimum **L**essons.

Much easier to remember, don't you think? If we remember the phrase 'Really what's necessary are optimum lessons' (which would be quite easy to do), we'll automatically have the first letters of our key words — RWNAOL.

Because we've arranged the material in our brains through a logical, sequential process — remember the filing cabinet concept? — we can now retrieve the words: *recall, writing, notetaking, advertising, oral presentations, listening.* And, since we've stored the information through a systematic process, we're in good shape to relate the words to the ideas that were expressed.

Throw in the filler words and, bingo, we're right back where we started, as illustrated in Figure 7:

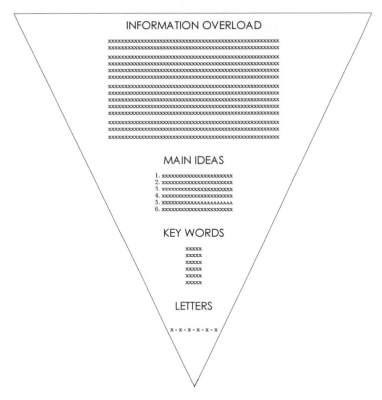

Fig. 7 • The Process Of Chunking

What chunking does, then, is transform the complex into the simple. It's an active learning process that stores meaningful information in a way that can successfully be recalled later. If the process seems, at first glance, to be more trouble than just reading the paragraph over and over, just consider how much of the paragraph would have been learned using that standard tried-and-true method of rote memorization.

Applying the principle of chunking <u>does</u> require a little more effort...

THAT'S WHY IT WORKS.

BRAIN WAVES

15. Emotion

As has been mentioned a number of times already — sorry, but I just can't emphasize this enough — dull, colourless, humdrum information has just a minimal chance of being very easily or quickly stored in our brains.

In fact, survey after survey of successful learning experiences all around the world consistently find one common ingredient, one characteristic factor that makes each and every one of them effective. No matter what format or style or particular strategy is used, each one of these successful learning experiences has, at its core, the element of *emotion*.

Emotional hooks powerfully embed information in our heads, and those hooks latch onto the right side of the brain. That's why we often recall events in our lives that have affected our hearts, but we rapidly lose track of the ones that don't.

My grandmother lived to the ripe old age of 96 years old. She spent the last few years of her life being cared for in a nursing home, where I visited her weekly. On one such occasion, as I entered her room, an orderly was in the process of clearing away her lunch tray. As he left the room, I said to her: "So what did you have to eat for lunch today?"

She looked at me, thought about it for a minute, and told me that she couldn't remember what she'd eaten. And I could see that she was visibly upset that she couldn't recall what she'd just eaten mere minutes before I'd entered the room.

In an effort to calm her down, I changed the subject and began discussing various family matters. Soon, she asked me if she'd ever told me how she and my grandfather had met. When I said that I'd never heard that story, she launched into quite a lengthy account of that special day in both their lives. She told me how she had been a nurse assigned to a hospital in London, England during the First World War, and he was a soldier stationed in some barracks nearby.

But she didn't simply give me a general outline of how they'd met. She painted a vivid picture of that day their paths had crossed: where they were, what they were wearing, what time of day their paths had crossed, what the weather was like, etc. And this was an event that had occurred over 70 years before!

Because it was such an important event in her life, and because of the strong emotional ties she had to that day's events, this woman in her 90s — the same person who minutes earlier couldn't even remember what she'd just eaten for lunch — now appeared to have a brain just as robust and as capable of effective memory skills as anyone I'd ever known.

Again, because so much information we deal with on a day-to-day basis is not on its own particularly fascinating, we really should try extra hard to make every effort possible to 'dress up' uninteresting material somehow. Only then will that material become more memorable and successfully learned.

When we use lifeless vocabulary, predictable clichés, wordy sentences and lengthy paragraphs — and then present them in a tired and dated format — we flirt with a guaranteed brain disaster.

Nothing will put us to sleep faster and deeper, not to mention impede attention and understanding more certainly, than learning and communicating in this fashion.

As a result, any emotional hook that we can think of that will create extra interest should be considered. Using lively language, variety in sentence structure and length, highlighted sections, bulleted lists, shapes and colours — all these strategies can contribute to an enticing learning package that will most definitely appeal to the sensuous nature of our brains.

In summary: Using all seven of the previously mentioned brain-training basics in combination takes the process of learning to heights rarely achieved by most of us whose ability to use our brains exceptionally well has been seriously held back by our prior lack of training. These principles boost our ability not only to perform the fairly mundane (but, nevertheless, often important) tasks in life, but also to achieve success in situations that can have great impact on our lives. They provide us with a framework that matches the way our brains actually operate, so we can remember people's names well, write dynamic reports, prepare powerful presentations, design impressive résumés and achieve sparkling test results.

These basics apply to all learning situations. Employing every one of the seven collectively — not choosing just one or two of them because they're easy to use — will transform our ability both to learn and to communicate successfully.

BRAIN WAVES

BRAIN ADVENTURES

*I felt that I now understood what learning is.
Of course, learning can be like looking up the
meaning of a word. That's learning for sure,
sort of like planting a blade of grass in a lawn.
But then there's the kind of learning that's like
dynamiting the whole lawn and starting over.*

Julie Gerchak in *My Ishmael* by Daniel Quinn

16. Brain Glue

Time to recap. Earlier in the book, I was the bearer of a considerable amount of bad news. Here's a list of the numerous impediments to learning that have been mentioned so far:

The rate of change is constantly accelerating.

Information overload is overwhelming us.

Boring material bounces right off our heads.

*Our brains operate much faster than
the rate that information comes in.*

Lack of effort impedes successful learning.

*We tend to forget more than half of what
we learn within an hour of learning it.*

Passive learning is often ineffective.

*Our short-term memories hold around
seven items for only 30 seconds or so.*

*Our long-term memories input information
slowly and don't always file material properly.*

*The traditional emphasis on left-brain skills
can throttle creative thought processes.*

There are, though, simple techniques and strategies that can help us overcome these problems. Making an effort to balance our brains by strengthening our weak-side skills is one way to breathe new life into our heads, and attending to the seven brain-training basics creates a semblance of order where there has too often been chaos in our thought processes.

What else can we do to use our brains better, smarter and faster? Whether we're the ones trying to access and understand information or the ones whose intention it is to communicate information to others, there are a few elementary stages in any learning system that will help us make new knowledge stick.

Making something memorable is much more than a case of constant repetition in a left-brain manner. But it's also not just simply 'dressing it up' using right-brain methods either.

Actually, as was suggested in Chapter 6, using our heads to their full potential requires us to combine the talents of *both* sides of the brain, a meshing of the logical reasoning prowess of the left side and the creative and sensual nature of the right side. It's the collaboration of the two sides that leads most astonishingly, yet inevitably, to intense brainpower.

Much of what we read is presented in small black print, white background, plain font, long sentences, paragraph form. Word after word, line after line, paragraph after paragraph, page after page, document after document.

As a steady diet, it's not very appetizing to look at, that's for sure. And guess what your brain often does when it sees this? *It tries to run away and hide.*

And guess what your heart does when it sees it? Well, let me put it this way: *It sure isn't falling in love!* And the problem exists not only when information is presented this way in written form. The same applies if it's offered verbally. (I don't know about you, but I've never found listening to someone read from a script terribly appealing or engaging.)

Something has to be done about this. Again, whether we're the ones presenting the information or the ones whose job it is to wade through it, the way the material is presented has an awful lot to do with the prospect of its being paid attention to, remembered and learned. What to do? One way to tackle this issue is to execute the following three-step plan:

ORGANIZATION

CHUNKS

IMAGINATION

To make material understandable and learnable, we need to make the effort to translate the way information is often given to us into a meaningful and memorable package.

Organizing it into chunks and then adding the quality of imagination is the perfect recipe for success. For instance, we should avoid the belief that repetitive reading is, on its own, significantly useful. Reading a passage over and over for, let's say, half an hour isn't a very efficient way to learn it. Rather than doing that, it would be much wiser to spend half the time — 15 minutes — reading it once slowly but *actively*.

This is where highlighting would make sense. And, once we've identified the main ideas and the pertinent details, we should then actively begin the translation process, modifying the left-brain material that's been presented to us and transforming its format into a more visually appealing and brain-friendly layout, like so:

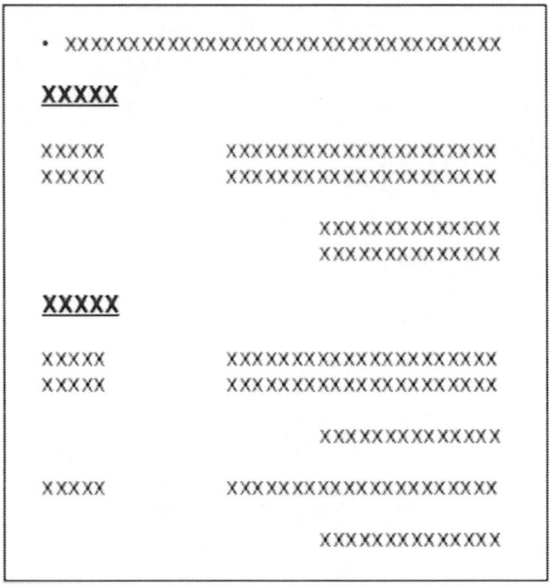

Fig. 8 • Much Better!

Repetitive reading is a waste of time for a variety of reasons. It takes too long, for one thing. It requires us to spend as much time on words like "of" and "from" and "the" as we do on the important words. We keep rereading the parts we already understood in the first place. And we continue to go over the parts we don't even really have to know.

Figure 8 presents an alternative method that requires more effort, but for good reason. It works! Changing a passage so that it's organized into chunks is an essential component of the process of learning.

A complaint I sometimes hear is that this kind of technique is too much trouble — that, if we have to do all this work, we won't have any time left to actually learn the material. This sentiment, however, is the exact opposite of the truth. The point is that reading and rereading basically shuts down the brain, making the time and effort expended on that method of learning next to useless. Here's the reality:

• It's *because* breaking down information into chunks requires effort that it's a useful strategy.

• It's *because* our brains have to think about and consider the words and ideas offered that we'll comprehend the material and remember it later.

• It's *because* this translation process forces us to weigh and evaluate what we read that our brains pay attention.

Actively organizing information into chunks is necessary. Period.

Consider the following example that should put what I'm saying into perspective. Let's say you're interested in applying for a new position, and the first step in the job-hunting process is attaining an interview, so you sit down to prepare a résumé. What's it going to look like?

I'm guessing that you'd design your résumé somewhat along the lines of the format suggested in Figure 8. And why is that? Why wouldn't you, instead, just print out a few pages describing your life story in paragraph form?

The answer to that question, of course, is that nobody would want to read it. It would be too long, too dense, too boring and too time-consuming. If you were the recipient of such a résumé yourself, you might just decide to direct it straight from the envelope into the wastebasket.

Here's what seems strange, then: This example makes absolutely perfect sense to just about everybody when considered in light of the way résumés look, yet these very same people seem hopelessly committed to using ineffective layout formats when composing so much of their other writing.

It's as if we think that résumés are important, but memos, letters, e-mail messages, reports and study notes are not.

Résumés are organized into chunks because we want to glance at them as quickly as possible and find particular information easily. We don't want to have to search for what we're looking for; we want it to leap out at us. But when we write something with little regard for its visual impact, it's like sending someone to look for a ping-pong ball in a thick, overgrown jungle using a machete to clear the way. It's difficult. It's frustrating. It's aggravating.

So why do we do it? Because it doesn't require a lot of effort on our part. Because it's not too much trouble. And, of course, that's why it's so ineffective.

In truth, doesn't this seem a particularly foolish strategy to use when we write? If we're going to spend the time and effort communicating with others, why take a course of action that's almost guaranteed to lead our readers directly down the path to weak comprehension and poor recall? If we're going to communicate, shouldn't we instead try to do it in a way that's actually effective and worthwhile?

According to Joyce Wycoff in her book, *Mindmapping*, here are the three maxims of writing:

1. Nobody wants to read it.

2. Hardly anyone will read all of it.

3. Most people will misunderstand some part of it.

I don't think too many of us would dispute these sentiments. But it's unwise to ignore this issue by simply shrugging it off as just "the way it is". As information providers, we should take this knowledge and correct the problems associated with traditional writing by helping our readers deal effectively with what we have to say.

OK, now let's move on to the third way to make information more memorable.

BRAIN WAVES

17. Brain Tricks

What's the the third way to make information brain-friendly? *Imagination.*

As mentioned earlier, it's interest that arouses the brain, helps it focus attention and keeps it awake. No matter how well material is organized into manageable chunks, our brains will tune out pretty quickly unless there's something there that acts as a hook. And it's imagination that provides that hook.

This isn't to say that the passage illustrated in Figure 8 (p. 146) isn't a tremendous improvement over what normally passes for a standard document's look. It is, unquestionably. But, without adding imagination, it's still not enough to grab our readers' attention.

So we have to work a little harder and dig a little deeper to figure out some way to improve the material that we create. And the best place to find our hook, of course, would be in the right-brain attributes that create a party atmosphere inside our heads.

Any one of those traits will bolster the good job we've already done by organizing the original document into chunks. If it's true that no one will read the whole passage, then we might as well influence our readers by focusing their attention on what we think is important.

Two such factors that would make an immediate impact are shape and design. You must admit that shape and design have a fairly dramatic way of attracting attention. As soon as our eyes hit the page, they're instantly drawn to the appearance and the words associated with them, as shown in Figure 9:

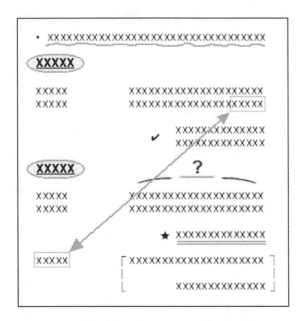

Fig. 9 • The Addition Of Shape & Design

Here's something else to consider: *Colour markers aren't just for little kids.* Colour appeals to adult brains just as it does to children's brains. Adding shape and design and colour adds the property of imagination to organization and chunks, and this addition completes our three-part mission. You might want to think of this as a trick that we play on the brain.

No matter how dry the material and how much its content keeps our brains at a distance, tricks like using shape and design will most often ignite enough interest to keep our audience reading. And keeping them reading, of course, should be the goal of all of us who engage in written communication with others.

When the shoe is on the other foot, however, and we're the ones who are now having to read material that hasn't been organized into imaginative chunks, then we simply reverse the process. Active reading involves applying the same strategies, but *as we read* rather than as we write.

Since most people haven't been well trained to learn and so aren't even aware of the commonly brain-deadening nature of most traditionally written communication, then we have to take it upon ourselves to do the translation on our own: taking what's offered, organizing it, forming chunks of information and tricking our brains into paying attention by adding shape and design.

Too much trouble? Hardly. Too time-consuming? Not really. Useful? For sure.

Another trick we can use is something we played around with as children and then, unfortunately, often forgot about when we got a bit older. To use a previous example, ask any Grade 9 student (even one who is academically weak) for the order of operations in math, and this is the response you're bound to get: BEDMAS.

Not many students, of course, would easily have learned the lengthy version: *brackets, exponents, division, multiplication, addition, subtraction.* It's a long list (almost seven items), and the words' order seems meaningless.

Using first letters of words to make up a word or phrase is called mnemonics. Another example from the world of mathematics is SOHCAHTOA, which is a made-up word that provides a simpler way to remember this formula: *sin(O/H)cos(A/H)tan(O/A)*. Who would remember that easily without a trick?

As was suggested back in Chapter 11, you can use mnemonics to incorporate the technique of association to assist learning and remembering. An example: I once delivered a presentation to a group of about 100 retired businesspeople, most of whom were in their 70s and 80s. When I asked if any of them knew the notes on the treble-clef scale in music, I was quite surprised to discover that almost all of them remembered that the five notes on the scale are E-G-B-D-F.

Now, these were businesspeople, not musicians — yet most of them remembered something taught to them early in their elementary school years. The reason for their shockingly good memories, in this instance, is that they didn't merely learn the five notes in sequence, because that wouldn't have worked very successfully, certainly not so well that they'd remember the list several decades later.

What they did learn was a phrase — probably *Every Good Boy Deserves Fudge* — made up of words whose first letters represented each of the notes. Oddly, literally millions of people on the face of this planet know what these notes are, even though they've probably never actually needed to know them.

We can remember many other lists using mnemonic devices, including the Great Lakes (HOMES: *Huron, Ontario, Michigan, Erie, Superior*) and the colours of the rainbow (ROY G. BIV: *Red, Orange, Yellow, Green, Blue, Indigo, Violet*).

There's no reason we should stop using these kinds of tricks as we age. As a matter of fact, because we have to learn and remember more and more as we get older, we probably should use mnemonics even more.

While it's true that mnemonics can be used to remember information to be learned at school and at work, it's also a fact that they can also be very handy for all kinds of day-to-day tasks we so often deal with: grocery lists, computer passwords, names of the members of a group, etc.

Some have suggested to me that they're uncomfortable having to rely on tricks to remember information. They find it embarrassing, they say, that they can't remember the information without help. But there really should be no shame attached to the use of tricks. After all, it's not necessarily an admission of an old, failing memory; it's simply an easy and painless way to help our brains hang onto information!

So next time you have to learn something — particularly if it's long, dry and complex — make an effort to organize the material into imaginative chunks. You just might be surprised at the results.

BRAIN WAVES

18. A Good Idea

I'd like to share with you a technique that's been around for a long time. And then, subsequently, I'll suggest a way to update it so it's even more relevant to the present day. It's a method of reading that's been included in just about every book about learning I've ever read, yet it's an active brain strategy that's unknown to most people. It's called SQ4R.

SQ4R is a mnemonic that stands for a six-step plan that's guaranteed to ensure faster reading with improved concentration, comprehension and recall. Its effectiveness has been proven many times over by a multitude of research studies.

It's too bad then, given all the reading that so many of us have to do these days, that so few of us leave school knowing anything at all about it. It even incorporates all seven of the brain-training basics pointed out earlier in this book. SQ4R stands for the following:

SURVEY

QUESTION

READ

RECITE

RECORD

REVIEW

SURVEY

Before we drive somewhere we've never been to before, we need directions. And the easiest way to plan the trip is to first consult a map. A map will tell us where we're starting out, what direction we need to travel, which places we'll pass through along our journey, where we'll finally arrive and approximately how long the trip will take.

Few of us would embark on such an excursion without first finding out this kind of information. In fact, we'd be foolish not to prepare ourselves in this way before beginning the trip.

Yet this is exactly what most of us do before beginning to read. In fact, to prepare to read a long and difficult document, whether it be a report, a journal article or a textbook chapter, we generally... *do nothing at all*. Rather, we open it up to the first page, take a deep breath and start reading — just the way we'd do if it were a novel we were planning to read for pleasure. (Except without the pleasure.)

Because we begin most of our reading journeys without first consulting a map, it's no wonder that we so often reach our destinations with such little knowledge of where we've traveled.

Surveying is like looking at a map before heading out. Sometimes called prereading, it's a quick process that involves following three simple instructions:

1. Read the introduction.

2. Look at the headings.

3. Read the summary.

The very little time that surveying takes prepares us for the task ahead by showing us where we're starting out, what direction we're going, which ideas we'll come across along the way, where we'll end up, and approximately how long it will take to read the material.

Doing this will take all of a few minutes in most cases since there's no pressure to actually learn or remember this information. All we're doing, really, is getting ready for the trip.

And now we're ready for Step #2.

QUESTION

As we take note of each heading, we quickly form a question in our minds, using the words the heading has given to us — along with who, what, where, when, why or how.

For instance, a heading such as *The Five Character-istics Essential For Success* would most likely lead to a question like 'What Are The Five Characteristics Essential For Success?' We don't have to write these questions down; we just mentally consider them as we read each heading.

What this does is alert our brains to the basic content of what we're going to read. These questions immediately send messages to the brain to be pro-cessed on a subconscious level so that, as soon as the questions are asked, our brains start looking through their filing systems for more information.

As a result, our brains will make predictions of the correct answers. But whether or not we come up with the correct predictions is beside the point.

The fact is that we're now paying attention to what we're reading, both focusing our attention on the main ideas and forcing our brains to work a little bit. This basic technique of questioning as we survey takes very little time, yet it will be responsible for considerably increasing the rate of the upcoming reading process and will lead to vastly improved comprehension.

READ

Now it's time to read. Thanks to the two previous steps, of course, reading will immediately be easier and faster.

For one thing, we have a purpose for reading in that we have some idea of what we're looking for. Aimlessly wandering through the material (as we'd meander along the roads if we didn't first check a map) is frustrating and would take too much time as we'd sometimes have to loop back to check where we've been.

But now we have questions that need answers. So, as we read, our job is to search for the answers to the questions we formed from the headings. We know where we're going — and we have a plan!

RECITE

There's no point in continuing to Part B if we didn't understand Part A. Reciting involves making sure, before jumping further ahead, that we came up with decent answers to our prior questions. Without good comprehension of each section of the material, the material that follows won't make as much sense, and our minds might drift off. So it's a form of verification, a check to make sure that we're still on the right track.

RECORD

This is the step that particularly addresses the concept of active learning that's so important to the brain's processing abilities.

It's very important to remember that organizing information into chunks is the way our brains like to work best. That's the reason why we should always try to get into the habit of reading one section at a time rather than trying to synthesize pages and pages of information all at once and overloading our short-term memory systems.

As we finish each section of the material we're reading, we need to get into the habit of stopping and giving our brains an opportunity to absorb what we've read so far. The best way to do this — the most *active* way to do this — is to stop and record the main points before moving on.

The way that this is done is completely up to each individual. We should select a technique that works for us and suits our own particular learning style, whether it be highlighting, making margin notes or transferring key thoughts and ideas onto a separate piece of paper or an audio recording.

The main thing to remember is that we must stop after each section and try to assimilate the information we've read, even though this might slow us down a bit. Slowing down is worth it, in this case, because we're really only using the time we previously gained by working through the previous steps.

Overall, and this seems to come as a surprise to many who try it, we're still reading the passage faster than we normally would. And we're retaining more.

REVIEW

The final phase of the SQ4R process is review. If the first step (SURVEY) was like looking at a map before proceeding on a journey, then reviewing is stopping at the end of the trip and looking back at the route we've taken. And, like surveying, this last step involves the same three instructions:

1. Read the introduction (again).
2. Look at the headings (again).
3. Read the summary (again).

While surveying is a form of prereading, reviewing could be called **post**reading. Unfortunately, many people question the need for this last step.

As a matter of fact, some who try the SQ4R process for the first time claim that their reading experience is already so enhanced that it seems unnecessary to bother with reviewing at this point. Why go to the trouble of doing it, they say, if they've already comprehended the material so well?

Well, here's the point: In most cases, as soon as we finish reading a document, the material immediately begins to withdraw. The information hasn't quite stuck in our minds yet, so some of the memory traces promptly start to exit the brain.

Mere comprehension of the content isn't enough. We also need to store the material so that we can recall it later, and adding this final review step to SQ4R stems the outward flow of information and strengthens the memory traces.

SQ4R is one of the best methods for reading and remembering ever devised. Its step-by-step process practically ensures success and should be taught to young people everywhere to prepare them for the reading tasks that await them later in life. It's a proven strategy backed by solid research.

If we had long ago been apprised of the benefits of such a strategy, if SQ4R had been drilled into our heads early on when we were first learning how to learn, imagine how much less stressful the reading demands in our lives today would be!

But I have to admit that hardly anyone uses it. Of the thousands of people I've presented it to, probably just a small number have wholeheartedly embraced it.

Why? Because they think it's too much trouble. (It's not, really, once you get used to the process. And, anyway, it's making the effort that helps contribute to the successful result.) Or it's too time-consuming. (This is an absolute misconception. The truth is that the six steps actually take *less* time than the slow, inefficient one-step reading most of us presently engage in.)

Luckily, though, there's a way to take the benefits of SQ4R and repackage them into a modern, updated format so that the process is much more enticing and better suited to our needs in today's information-laden world.

BRAIN WAVES

19. A Great Idea

One method of organizing information, and a practical alternative to SQ4R that's been implemented by a number of private and public organizations, is called the Fish Bones diagram, because its format somewhat resembles the skeleton of a fish, as illustrated in Figure 10 below:

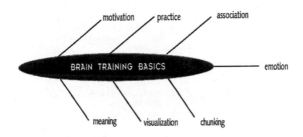

Fig. 10 • Fish Bones – Part Three of The Big Learn

This format adheres to the basic understanding that it's usually a good idea to present information visually and in an imaginative, non-linear way. Personally, I find the fish bones idea quite interesting, but perhaps a bit limiting in that it doesn't leave an awful lot of room for details and examples.

Over the years, many variations of this particular kind of organizational model (sometimes called concept mapping) have been designed. What is generally considered to be the original prototype, though, was devised by Tony Buzan.

One of Buzan's revelations concerns an approach that he calls mindmapping. It's his contention that recording information in a linear format, as we've been trained to do, is counterproductive to the ways our thinking patterns function.

Buzan's mindmaps resemble the constitution of brain cells, with a core at the nucleus (the primary concept) surrounded by dendrite-like branches of information (the main ideas and details). Figure 11 provides an example of a mindmap:

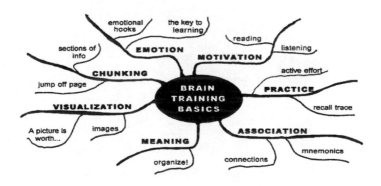

Fig. 11 • Mindmap – Part Three of The Big Learn

The essence of the various versions of Buzan's original concept remain the same. All offer simple, learner-friendly alternatives both to the process of left-brain, linear transcription and to the SQ4R process.

Generally, the point of mapping is that, in order for our brains to engage in successful learning experiences, information needs to be expressed with attention paid to several combinations of factors — *all* the concepts — discussed in previous chapters.

The linear brain skills that we've been encouraged to strengthen over the years have, unfortunately, very little to do with these concepts, though. Mapping, on the other hand, recognizes and attends to every single one of the principles referred to in this book.

Mapping is so simple and so common-sense a notion that it's really a mystery why this dynamic and creative solution to the kinds of problems we face with disseminating, organizing and learning information hasn't been more regularly put into practice.

It addresses many issues we face in the various dimensions of our personal, social, academic and workplace lives, and it can be applied at both the micro and the macro levels of what we do. Its use is multidisciplinary. It can be employed before, during and after learning situations, whether the tasks involve thinking, problem-solving, listening, writing or reading.

For instance, creating a map before attempting to read a 50-page document would guarantee faster reading, better comprehension and vastly improved recall. And the bare bones of such a premap can be devised with minimal initial effort because the task requires little more than jotting down only those features of the text which leap off the page, leaving the details to be filled in later as the reader goes through the material more carefully.

I prefer to call this kind of visual representation of linearly offered material (reports, manuals, textbooks) 'brainmapping'. An effective brainmap embraces all of what we know about how to supercharge our minds. Figure 12 presents an example of a brainmap that does just that:

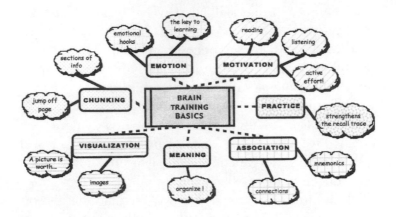

Fig. 12 • Brainmap – Part Three of The Big Learn

Please understand that brainmapping is absolutely true to the many ways our brains actually perform, as illustrated in every chapter of this book so far:

Designing a brainmap depends on interest, attention and effort. (Chapter 1)

Its creation is an active learning process requiring both mental and physical involvement. (Chapter 2)

It helps transfer information from short-term to long-term memory. (Chapter 3)

It includes tricks that help store facts into our memory banks. (Chapter 4)

It pays heed to the active involvement techniques suggested by the Cone of Learning. (Chapter 5)

It acknowledges the research dealing with strategies to increase dendrite growth. (Chapter 6)

It's a balanced-brain process, combining left-brain material like words and numbers with right-brain elements like shapes and images. (Chapter 7)

Its design is compatible with 'the perfect brain environment'. (Chapter 8)

It incorporates all seven brain-training basics by relying on motivation, practice, association, meaning, visualization, chunking and emotion. (Chapters 9 through 15)

It forces us to organize information spatially. (Chapter 16)

It requires imagination. (Chapter 17)

It can be easily adapted to embrace the proven principles of SQ4R. (Chapter 18)

To be honest with you, it took me quite some time myself to understand and appreciate one of the most utilitarian applications of brainmapping, and that is its use as a precursor to mindful reading. And here's why that's such a very good idea: It allows us to *start and stop* on an ongoing basis.

What I mean by that is that it addresses the problem that most of us have of rarely, if ever, being able to take the opportunity to actually focus our attention for any appropriate length of time on multi-page documents.

Realistically, how often can most of us set aside
two or three continuous hours out of a day to devote to
such tasks?

We keep looking for that elusive amount of free
time which we'll be able to use to focus on reading the
document, but usually with little luck. And we certainly
don't relish the idea of starting to read it if we know
that we'll be interrupted or that we won't be able to
complete the reading, because we know that we
probably won't remember its content for long under
those kinds of circumstances.

So we put it off. And we put it off. And we put it off.

What I call 'premapping' eliminates this problem.
Once we've prepared a rudimentary premap beforehand
and, later on, find we have only 20 or so uninterrupted
minutes available to read, then we can simply devote
that time to reading the first section of the document
(perhaps just a handful of pages) and adding the cogent
details to the map as we do so.

Later in the day, if we find a bit more time to get
back to it, we can quickly read over what we jotted
down last time and add a bit more. The next day, or
the day after that, we can continue the process.

After several abbreviated sessions such as this, we'll
find that the job is done, and not only have we been
able to start and stop as we've been reading the
document, but now we have the added bonus of having
transformed the original premap into a full-fledged
brainmap — an easy-to-read balanced-brain summary
of its content at our disposal for review.

If you like this idea so far, then I hope you'll consider taking it one step further and make...

BRAIN-TRAINING WALLPAPER

Here's the idea: Find a big sheet of paper (2′ by 3′ would do the trick nicely), get out your colour markers and claim a big piece of floor space somewhere. It's time to create a large-scale version of your brainmap in as dynamic, creative and stimulating a way as you can muster.

The process of doing this is, first of all, an active means of reinforcing the key concepts and the important details of the document you're working with. And, of course, it's an enjoyable experience, too. (So you should probably also play some music while you're doing it, just to make sure the right side of your brain is playfully engaged.)

Once done, you have something resembling a poster that can be mounted on a wall in a location where it will be easily seen and often noticed. Place it somewhere, for instance, where you can look at it while talking on the phone or doing busywork. Hang it up on the wall across from your desk at work, over the kitchen table, above the television, near your computer — even on the ceiling above your bed, if that suits you.

I remember when my son, Luke, entered high school. Like most kids his age, he hadn't in his previous years as a student been fully trained by the school system (or, I'm sorry to say, by me) to 'learn how to learn' and was, as a result, quite unprepared for the homework and studying demands of Grade 9.

As the end of his first high school semester was approaching and he was closing in on his first taste of final exams, it was obvious that he could use some guidance, especially with his History course, which he found confusing.

Mapping was a fairly new concept to me at the time, and I hadn't yet had much experience with it myself, but I figured it was worth a try. So we found nice big sheets of paper, grabbed a variety of markers, put some music on and sat down together to design simple premaps of each of the four textbook chapters that he was to be tested on. It would then be his job to go through the chapters and his notes and create more comprehensive brainmaps by filling in the details and examples that he'd need to know for the exam.

He told me later that this hadn't really seemed like studying to him. In fact, he was worried that all this 'doodling' was wasting the precious time that he needed to prepare for the exam! But — more as a favour to me than anything else, I think — he went to work.

Once he'd completed the brainmaps, we hung each one up in various places around the house where he couldn't help but notice them. Over the course of the next couple of weeks, he perused them plenty of times until the information had sunk in pretty well, so he began to feel ready to be tested on the material. But he wasn't finished yet.

The night before the exam, he wallpapered the bathroom with the four brainmaps, plugged in his music player to listen to some tunes he liked, and filled the tub for a nice, relaxing soak. And, in this unconventional way, he crammed for the exam.

So guess what happened? He achieved the best mark he'd ever gotten to that point in his life as a student. And, to this day, this is his preferred method of learning.

Why should we go to such lengths to train our brains? And why should we share these ideas not just with young people but with adults as well? Because our adult brains operate the same way as they did when we were children, that's why.

Remember this: We're often amazed at how Grade 2 children — *those little learning sponges!* — absorb so much information so quickly and with such apparent ease. Well, it's no wonder, is it?

In your mind's eye, take a look again at the perfect brain environment in which young children usually learn — visual stimulation all over the place, left-brain material learned with the help of the right side of the brain — and compare those surroundings and those strategies to the gray, cubicle-world atmosphere and the traditionally tedious techniques we so often design for ourselves as adult thinkers and learners.

We'd all do our brains an immense favour if we'd borrow from the learning environments and experiences we so wisely try so hard to establish for young minds. We should recreate grown-up versions of them for ourselves in order to invigorate and activate our own adult minds.

Brain-training wallpaper is an excellent example of how we can do just that.

BRAIN WAVES

NO TRAIN — NO GAIN

*The illiterate of the future won't be those
who cannot read and write, but those
who cannot learn, unlearn and relearn.*

Alvin Toffler

20. Brains At School

Learning to use our brains better has a multitude of functions that can be employed in various situations that we experience in our lives. Certainly, of course, it has relevance to the way we perform in school.

What's interesting, too, is that brain training can be applied at all academic levels. It's appropriate not only for children in the primary and junior grades, but it's also significant for adolescents in high school, students in college and university, and adults taking night school courses or training programs in the workplace.

Perhaps surprisingly, it's been suggested that post-secondary students who achieve the highest grade-point averages often spent less time studying per day than students who fail. This doesn't mean that studying is a bad idea. What it does suggest is that, when we use our brains inefficiently, our chances for success in school are severely limited — no matter how much time and effort we devote to the task.

Remember the Curve of Forgetting in Chapter 2? Dr. Hermann Ebbinghaus, so many years ago, proved that passive learning leads to an almost immediate loss of information, leaving only about 20% of the material (material that had already supposedly been learned) still remembered a full month after learning something new.

Above all, people in new learning situations must be acutely aware of the importance of the role that active learning plays. Its effectiveness has been proven over and over in one study after another.

If I were in school myself right now, I'd stick a copy of the Cone of Learning (Chapter 4) on my bathroom mirror and stare at it every time I brushed my teeth, constantly trying to think of new ways to apply its conclusions to whatever I was studying at the time.

What the research suggests is that the further we distance ourselves from passive learning like reading and listening, and the closer we push ourselves toward the opposite end of the scale to become more actively involved in the process, the more likely we are to learn and remember — both better and faster.

The more senses we use, the better our brains work. So it follows that anything we do that involves our brains on a sensual level is apt to be a good thing. Writing things down, saying things aloud, seeing visually stimulating representations of facts and figures and statistics, physically acting out new learning — all these activities will motivate our brains to function much closer to peak performance levels.

It's essential that we're aware of this kind of research, because understanding its implications will point us in the right direction when we're faced with having to prepare for tests and exams in academic environments. Let's face it, the testing process is what does so many of us in. Many students are quite capable of performing well in classroom settings, but it's exam time that often unravels whatever successes they've achieved over the course of a semester.

In the pressure-cooker atmosphere in which exams are held, many smart people fail primarily because they lack the knowledge of how their brains most easily organize, store and retain material.

There are a number of simple techniques that students should use, not only to achieve better test results, but also to save time that can be used for more enjoyable pursuits. These methods should be applied not just at the last minute on the night before the big test, but as an ongoing learning process beginning on the first day of school, in the classroom and at home.

IN CLASS

One of the biggest mistakes students make is to play a passive role while sitting in class. Granted, much of what takes place in the typical classroom scores pretty low on the scale of Fascinating Stuff To Do.

Nevertheless, proficient learners get past that. If their goal is to achieve good marks, then they realize that effort must be applied to work through the sometimes boring experiences that are bound to take place in an academic environment. Bear in mind that it's relatively easy to be successful with activities that interest us; it's in the ones that don't capture our imaginations that we most need to apply ourselves.

The first step is to develop a simple notetaking system. Since we're quite likely to forget much new information before we even exit through the classroom door, it's essential that we find some way to record material as it's first being introduced.

Whether we're listening to a teacher or reading a textbook, we can't just rely on our ears and eyes alone. We need to take notes with paper in front of us and markers in hand. The point is that we should make a record of what we're learning as soon as it's initially presented to us — or it will be quickly forgotten.

Those of us who feel most comfortable with a left-brain learning system should probably take notes along the lines of what's known as the Cornell Notetaking System, a technique that involves drawing a line about a third of the way over from the left side of the page. In the left-hand margin, we can write down the important points, saving the bulk of the space on the right side for the facts, the figures and the definitions.

Left-brainers will feel comfortable with the Cornell Notetaking System; it's not the least bit intimidating in a wild-and-crazy-artist kind of way. It has a neat, logical look to it and employs principles similar to those used when creating a résumé or a financial statement. A page designed with this system presents information in the kind of coherent top-to-bottom, left-to-right pattern that most of us have been exposed to through much of our lives.

To add just a touch of right-brain stimulation, it would be wise to think about adding some form of creative element to the page. Colour is an obvious choice. Many successful students use specific colour-coding systems to separate main ideas, secondary points, specific details, formulas, etc.

Another good idea would be to add shapes to make certain points stand out — for instance, rectangles could stand for one type of concept, triangles for another, circles for something else, etc. Any other tricks that can act as memory triggers, like pictures or quirky associative connections, should be added too. This will considerably enhance the likelihood of remembering information at a later date. Figure 13 illustrates an example of this type of notetaking:

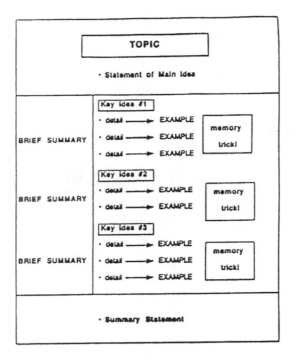

Fig. 13 • Good Left-Brain Notes

A more brain-friendly approach to notetaking, though, would likely involve something more akin to the brainmapping concept discussed in Chapter 19. The fundamental difference is to create a shift to right-brain features (like visualization through shape and design), bestowing the predominant role in the way the notes are organized to the brain's imaginative side. Rather than just presenting words, numbers and facts as the primary focus, these more inspired notes will attract the memory system's attention by stressing creative features, yet still in a logical and organized way.

This may not seem to be a terribly significant difference, but it is. After all, our brains work best when we're happy, and emotion is synthesized through the right side of the brain. Does it not make sense, then, to emphasize the more sensual nature of the thinking process by providing right-brain stimulation?

Figure 14 offers one way of doing this:

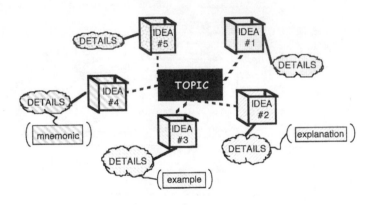

Fig. 14 • Good Balanced-Brain Notes

After notetaking, the next in-class strategy that I'd like to share is one that I can't emphasize too strongly:

ASK QUESTIONS!

This is something we spent a lot of time doing when we were younger and then too often stopped doing as we moved through the education system.

Why do we call young children 'learning sponges'? Because they learn so much and absorb information so quickly. And how do they accomplish this feat?

They pepper everyone they encounter with one question after another, that's how. "What's that for?", "What are you doing?", "How come?" and, of course, the never-ending "Why? Why? Why?" And the result is that they learn and they learn and they learn.

Probably the easiest and the fastest way to learn is to be placed in a situation that involves two-way communication, where we can ask for clarification as soon as something doesn't make sense to us. If we're still confused after hearing the answer, we can then ask for examples to help explain the concept. And we can continue asking questions until we finally understand.

But, as we get older, we don't spend nearly the amount of time asking questions as we did when we were younger. There are a variety of reasons for that but, first and foremost, here's the reason: *We don't want to look foolish in front of our peers.*

We want to ask questions, but we first take a look around the room and notice that everyone else seems to understand. (Often, in fact, our peers are most likely just acting like they know what's going on and would probably be extremely grateful if other people asked some questions on their behalf!)

I've long been a big fan of the Confucian saying that goes something like this: "It is better to ask a question and be a fool for five minutes than not ask and be a fool for a lifetime." Wise words, don't you think?

Of course, it's terribly unfortunate that every time we reject the face-to-face question-and-answer method of learning that works so quickly and so well — as we often do in many learning circumstances — we must then choose a weaker alternative to replace it.

Regrettably, in this case, there just aren't too many effective options available to us. The likely substitute, in fact, is to figure things out by reading the material later on in a textbook or report, which is arguably the most frustrating, aggravating and time-consuming way in the world to learn.

Think about it: Why would reading — a one-way process — be a superior method to asking questions? Communication experts tell us that there's just no better way to interact and learn than by engaging in face-to-face, two-way procedures. Enough said.

AT HOME

One of the biggest problems that students typically run into at school is falling behind with their homework. This is particularly serious for those who haven't paid enough attention in class and have developed neither a useful reading strategy nor an organized notetaking system, because now they have no safety net to help themselves catch up.

Without back-up systems, they dig themselves into pretty deep holes that can be awfully tough to crawl out of. Because they don't have decent notes (or often don't have notes at all), they have only textbooks to refer to. Because they didn't pay attention and ask questions in class, they have few reference points to access.

But, even if these areas have been addressed in the classroom, many falter once they're back in their home environment. Because of the left-brain attitudes that typically operate in our culture, most of us lack 'learning training' and so are woefully unprepared to face academic challenges on our own.

There are, though, some pretty basic steps that can be followed at home that can lead to vastly improved performance in school.

For instance, a common complaint of parents is that their children want to do homework while watching television. Naturally, this is a fairly legitimate gripe. However, there are some useful school-related activities that *can* take place in front of a TV — like going through binders, filing, organizing notes, and adding shape and design to the pages.

And using television time to create premaps is, for sure, an excellent idea. Going through a textbook chapter that hasn't yet been read and making a premap of headings, subheadings, boldface words, definitions and numbered lists is actually quite easy to do while sprawled out on the floor watching a favourite show. All that's needed, really, is a supply of large pieces of paper and markers. It doesn't even require a great deal of effort.

Once premaps have been created, remember, the material can then be approached on a start-and-stop basis — fifteen minutes before dinner, half an hour in the middle of the evening, an hour before going to bed. Once all the sections of the brainmap are completed, then it's time to use the final product as wallpaper in a popular area of the home.

If the perfect brain environment is the Grade 2 classroom, then why not apply the same principles to learning at home? So what if we decide to hang the brainmap above the television? If that's the place where we'll notice it most easily and most often, then that's where it should go!

For most of us (adolescents, certainly, but adults as well), there's no weaker brain strategy than associating learning with some kind of prison-like atmosphere. In other words, placing ourselves in a dull, quiet room and sitting on an uncomfortable chair under bright lights does little to stimulate either logical thinking or creative thought. In order to maximize the potential of our brains, we'd be wise to reshape the environment in which we choose to learn. Learning is a fascinating process; it shouldn't be viewed as torture.

Active learning in surroundings that stimulate the brain is good for us. Slowing down our brains through relaxation, or appealing to them by listening to music that we enjoy, has the potential to both calm and invigorate us and can generate absolutely terrific learning situations.

Decorating the walls of our homes with brain-training wallpaper, playing question-and-answer games with others, choosing music and connecting tunes to material we're trying to learn — these are all techniques we can use to give our brains a fighting chance to operate at optimal levels. The result?

MORE FUN

A BETTER ATTITUDE

GREAT MARKS

BRAIN WAVES

21. Brains At Work

The same principles that apply to improved performance at school also have many applications in the workplace. For instance, numerous enterprises in business, industry and the public sector today seem to be quite keen on referring to themselves as 'learning organizations'. Because there's been such a great deal of downsizing and restructuring over the past several years, it's now essential that employees of leaner enterprises have the capability to keep up with constant change by learning quickly and well.

In a presentation I once made to a large multi-national telecommunications firm, a supervisor told me the biggest issue being dealt with in that organization was that, by the time employees had completed one training program, it was already time to go directly into the <u>next</u> training program. There's so much to know, she said, and things are changing so fast!

Thomas L. Friedman agrees. In *The World Is Flat*, he says that "being adaptable in a flat world, knowing how to 'learn how to learn', will be one of the most important assets any worker can have."

So the strategies I've been suggesting that students use in the classroom and at home should also most certainly be applied in workplace situations as well. Just as young people attend classes, many adults spend time in meetings and conferences. And just as students must employ notetaking skills and questioning techniques in class, employees should apply the same kinds of methods on the shop floor and in the boardroom.

It's just as easy to drift off in a meeting and leave the room with little recollection of what exactly took place as it was when our minds wandered and we forgot course instruction in school.

Quite frankly, it's probably *more* important that we develop focusing skills at work. As students, if we failed, we could always just take the course over again. As employees, if we fail, we can actually get fired!

Most businesspeople these days keep track of their agendas through the use of some form of schedule planner, either paper or electronic. And why do they do this? Well, they do it because recording timetables, meetings, appointments, etc. is one of the ways we can adhere to the principle that we should keep the boring stuff outside of our heads.

Writing things down, for one, is an active process that tends to strengthen recall traces. (Have you ever noticed that, if you write a reminder note and put it in your pocket, you probably remember the note's content without ever having to refer to it?) As well, getting mundane information out of our heads and recorded somewhere else clears our brains, leaving more space for new data and creative thought.

It often happens that I'm approached by someone and asked to get together for a meeting or social event at some future date. When this occurs, I immediately take out my planner and take note of the person's name and the date, time and place of the suggested meeting.

This sometimes surprises, even confuses, them. Often, they say: "Hey, you're a brain guy! Why do you have to write it down? Surely you can just remember it in your head!"

Nope. Actually, it's <u>because</u> I'm a brain guy that I have to write it down. Otherwise, it's quite possible that I'm going to forget it. Just like everyone else, I need to use outside sources to record this kind of information.

We should also apply the principles of brain training to the many communication issues we face in the workplace. More than ever these days, we're required to communicate with others in different formats. While we used to contact others primarily through telephone calls, faxes, memos, letters and reports, we're now more often using e-mail and text-messaging.

Learning and communication skills are essential ingredients of workplace success, so the way we use them can obviously have a substantial impact on how we perform on the job.

First of all, the way we organize our time can make or break how much we accomplish on any given day. Staying on top of things is paramount to maximizing our potential. Using planners is one way we can achieve success in this area, but it's also necessary to apply organizational skills to the various tasks we engage in as we work.

One way to do this is to find ways to focus on the big things we need to do while dispensing with the little things as quickly and as efficiently as possible. Another way is to keep daily updated lists that indicate what's urgent, what's relatively important and what's not quite so pertinent to our immediate goals. By applying simple, active notetaking skills as we read material, for example, we can get many of those smaller tasks taken care of and out of the way.

Many professionals do this by simply writing notes directly on the documents they receive and sending them back immediately to the source, saving precious time that can be better used for the major issues they need to focus on.

What we ourselves write should follow the guidelines recommended earlier in this book, with attention paid not only to the words we choose but to the look of the documents as well. If our memos, letters and reports all look and sound exactly like everyone else's memos, letters and reports, it's unlikely that what we have to say will make a very powerful or memorable impression on those who are going to read what we have to say.

Many years ago, the late Malcolm Forbes wrote an article titled *How To Write A Business Letter*. One of the things he emphasized was that we should make our letters look appetizing. A prominent letterhead is a start. Organizing our words in a brain-friendly format is a good idea, too — not just with paragraphs but with the creative use of white space, borders and design.

The first maxim of business writing is, after all, that very few people actually want to read the stuff we write. Given that fact, it's essential that we do our best to make an effort to appeal somehow to our readers' senses, using whatever right-brain resources we can muster.

The second maxim is that very few will completely read what we've written, so perhaps we should consider adding colour and highlighting phrases — in fact, doing anything we can think of to direct attention to the points we want our readers to notice and attend to.

If they're not going to read the whole thing, then maybe we should do something to encourage them to be more aware of the key points we're trying to communicate. I mean, think about how you feel when you first pick up a 50-page report. On an emotional, right-brain level, what's your reaction? Are you dying to read it? Unlikely. So we must understand that others are likely to respond in exactly the same way when they encounter what *we* write.

Page after page of blah, blah, blah, blah, blah just doesn't cut it when communicating in today's work environment. So let's just accept the fact that anything we can do to motivate and stimulate our readers' brains will, in all likelihood, help to communicate our messages much more effectively.

And it's not just in our written communication that we can apply brain-training theories. It's common knowledge that one of the best ways to move up the corporate ladder is to develop exceptional speaking skills. If it's true that speaking in public is the #1 human fear, then it makes sense that one way to distance ourselves from the pack is to cultivate our ability to make dynamic presentations.

Again, the same principles that apply to reading and writing should be exercised when speaking. To be effective communicators, we can't just stand up and transmit facts. We must engage our audiences' hearts.

For one thing, because we're, for all intents and purposes, 'on stage' when we speak, we should give consideration to our visual impact. If it's our job to be leaders in the minds of others, then we should foster an appearance that elevates us in that respect.

Another way to create impact, aside from our own personal appearance, is to back up our words with images and illustrations — because words, numbers, facts and figures don't stick easily to brains on their own.

But just having some form of visual backup alone isn't enough. If the material, for instance, consists wholly of words and numbers on a plain background, we negate the possible impact that such material might have. To be true to the lessons learned from the Cone of Learning and to accommodate both the left and right sides of our listeners' brains, it makes sense that any visual representations we include in our presentations should be interesting and engaging.

That means using colour, including images along with textual material, and employing physical props. It means incorporating anything at all that we can think of to help others pay attention to the message we're presenting to them.

Another thing we really need to think about is group participation. Since it's so often been proven that the best way to encourage learning is to be involved in the process in some kind of interactive way, then it seems totally inappropriate to just 'talk at' people. Rather, we need to actually engage in two-way communication — either between speaker and audience or among group members themselves.

Remember that attention can be focused, at the best of times, in spurts of only about 20 minutes, so long presentations should be organized into chunks of approximately that length, alternating between a lecture style and more participative experiences.

Many people are afraid to speak in public because they're worried about potential embarrassment, about not doing well, or about the prospect of talking to others who might not be interested in listening to them. A left-brain format practically guarantees that those fears will, in fact, be realized. But balanced-brain strategies will have the opposite effect by connecting with listeners' hearts and minds at the same time.

As far as the initial process of organizing a presentation is concerned, let's go back to the mapping idea. Designing an initial premap of the information that's to be presented helps look after the preliminary process of organization. As with many tasks we face in life, it's the starting that's the tough part, and putting together a basic premap helps take care of that. If that premap is created on a large piece of paper and hung up in the office area (in plain view from a seat at a desk, for instance), then we'll find ideas easier to develop as we work through the process.

Compare this technique to setting aside a specific time, sitting down with pen in hand, and forcing ourselves to come up with great ideas on some kind of schedule. Too stressful! Too pressure-filled! Too brain-blocking! (Research suggests, by the way, that the best ideas evolve from relaxed discussions on breaks rather than during meeting-room conferences. A coincidence, do you think?)

Brainmaps aren't limited to the organization of presentations, of course. Just as lessons learned from the Grade 2 classroom environment should be followed by students working at home, so should they be observed in the workplace.

No matter who we are or what we're doing, one of the best ways to invigorate our brains and provoke them to work as magnificently as they're capable of operating is to pay attention to the list of seven brain-training basics. The creation of brainmaps addresses all these issues as well as paying heed to the kind of balanced-brain inspiration that's necessary to achieve success in whatever endeavour we're engaged in.

There are so many applications in the workplace! We can use brainmaps to prepare speeches, plan meetings, organize tasks for committees, write reports, develop marketing strategies and design advertising campaigns. We can use them to engage in problem-solving sessions, schedule events and prepare conference agendas.

The advantages of training our brains to achieve success in the workplace are virtually endless. It's easily worth the effort required and, in fact, will even save us a tremendous amount of time in the long run.

BRAIN WAVES

Afterword

Think left and think right and think low and think high.
Oh the thinks you can think up if only you try!
Dr. Seuss

It's more than just a shame that we haven't been more adept at quickly embracing the simple truths about our brains that have been discovered recently.

It's lamentable, too, that we haven't dutifully begun applying them to the ways we deal with the predicament of information overload that we face in our lives today. Really, it's a travesty.

Wherever I go and to whomever I'm introduced — young and old alike and from all walks of life — I keep hearing the same sad story: "I have too much to do, I don't have enough time to do it, and things are changing too fast."

It seems a great disservice to us all, and particularly to our youth, that we're not facing this dilemma head-on. Please understand: Some of this information is getting through, but only in dribs and drabs and for far too few people. In isolated classrooms, training facilities and corporate boardrooms, some progress is being made, but only to small special-interest groups of individuals here and there.

But that's not nearly enough, is it? Why on earth haven't these remarkable advances in brain training been, first of all, generally acknowledged and, more importantly, put into practice with a majority of those in the mainstream?

Of course, it's understandable that change takes time. And there's bound to be some resistance to the suggestion that the way we've been taught to use our brains in the past might be almost totally wrong. Given the fact that we've 'learned how to learn' using left-brain precepts and have received instruction almost exclusively from left-brainers who have themselves learned the same way, that's probably natural.

The truth is that the strongest left-brain thinkers in our society today have tended to assume the mantle of decision-making powers in most of our public and private institutions. They're leading and managing our schools, our organizations, our associations and our corporations. So it's obviously not an easy task to introduce innovative, balanced-brain measures that are likely to be automatically accepted with open arms by those who are entrusted with designing and implementing learning and training systems and programs.

There's no question that what we're talking about here is a full-scale, status-quo-challenging learning revolution. But we should realize too that, as our world is becoming more and more automated, there will soon come a point when the one thing for which human beings will be needed — and, more to the point, *valued* — will be our creative, balanced-brain skills.

It's true that separate ideas discussed in this book, when offered in isolation and lacking the context of the big picture (as is sometimes being done in schools and factories and corporations), might not have the impact necessary to harness a great deal of change on a widespread basis.

But now that you've been exposed to these ideas in the overall context of thinking and learning, I trust that you've come to understand that all the concepts that have been presented here are both interconnected and viable. Taken together as a whole, they really do make perfect sense.

So it's my hope that you're finishing this book with the revelation that your brain is much more powerful and adaptable than you ever realized and, more importantly, that you're perfectly capable of harnessing that potential to stretch the limits of your brainpower.

Taking heed of some fundamental truths about the brain and how it works has the potential to impact your life in a truly positive manner — leading to improved communication skills, enhanced problem-solving abilities, superior learning strategies and, ultimately, the kind of success that most people only dream about.

NOTES

01 • WHAT'S THE PROBLEM?

In *Mozart's Brain and the Fighter Pilot: Unleashing Your Brain's Potential* - New York: Three Rivers Press (2002), neuropsychiatrist Richard Restak combines the latest research in neurology and psychology to show us how to get brains up to speed for managing every aspect of our busy lives.

02 • THE PASSIVE LEARNING DEBACLE

For the original Curve of Forgetting research, see Dr. Hermann Ebbinghaus, *Memory, A Contribution to Experimental Psychology* - New York: Dover Publications (1987).

The website *www.freshpatents.com* provides some interesting background: "The history of learning psychology stems from the German psychologist Dr. Hermann Ebbinghaus (1850-1909). He specifically investigated the question of memory retention of information. Generally speaking, most forgetting occurs immediately after learning new material.

"In a famous set of experiments, Hermann Ebbinghaus tested his own memory at various times after learning. Ebbinghaus wanted to be sure he would not be swayed by prior learning, so he memorized different series of nonsense syllables. The meaningless 3 letter words, e.g., *fap, jis,* and *mib* were used to keep the learning experiments free of any correlation that could be made to previously attained knowledge. By waiting various lengths of time before testing himself, Ebbinghaus plotted the *Curve of Forgetting.*

"The following is an excerpt from the Ebbinghaus' book which was originally published in 1885. In this excerpt, Ebbinghaus relates his findings in the subsequent table, indicating values computed for the *Curve of Forgetting*:

"'It will probably be claimed that the fact that forgetting would be very rapid at the beginning of the process and very slow at the end should have been foreseen ... One hour after the end of the learning, the forgetting had already progressed so far that one half of the original work had to be expended before the series could be reproduced again; after 8 hours, the work to be made up was two thirds of the first effort.

"Gradually, however, the additional loss could be ascertained only with difficulty. After 24 hours, about one third was always remembered; after 6 days, about one fourth and, after a whole month, fully one fifth of the first work persisted in effect. The decrease of this after-effect in the latter intervals of time is evidently so slow that it is easy to predict that complete vanishing of the effect of the first memorization of these series would, if they had been left to themselves, have occurred only after an indefinitely long period of time.'"

For a practical application of the Curves of Forgetting & Remembering, see Transport Canada's 'Helicopter Flight Test Guides: Part I • Learning and Learning Factors' at this website: *www.tc.gc.ca/civilaviation/general/flttrain/Planes/Pubs/TP4818/PartI/Factors.htm*

03 • THE DILEMMA OF MEMORY

George A. Miller famously told us about the importance of the number seven in this article: *The Magical Number Seven, Plus or Minus Two: Some Limits on Our Capacity for Processing Information* - originally published in *The Psychological Review, 1956.*

04 • THE SUCCESSFUL BRAIN

From Wikipedia: "Tony Buzan (1942-) is the originator of mind mapping and coined the term 'mental literacy'. He was born in London and received double Honours in psychology, English, mathematics and the General Sciences from the University of British Columbia in 1964. He is probably best known for his book, *Use Your Head*, his promotion of mnemonic systems and his mind-mapping techniques.

"Following his 1970s series for the BBC, many of his ideas have been set into his series of five books: *Use Your Memory, Master Your Memory, Use Your Head, The Speed Reading Book* and *The Mind Map Book.*

"In essence, Buzan teaches 'learn how your brain learns rapidly and naturally'. His work is partly based on the explosion of brain research that has taken place since the late 1950s and the work on the left and right brain by Robert Ornstein and Roger Wolcott Sperry.

"Most of his teaching generally divides up into general awareness of the extensive capabilities and capacities of the brain and its functions; memory skills; reading skills; mind map note-taking; creativity; and how brain function can be improved over time into old age.

"Buzan developed Mind Mapping whilst at University, out of the frustration that traditional notes took up so much time to create and review. Research indicated that the brain responds best to key words, images, colours, and direct association. Buzan refined these ideas into a simple set of rules that can be followed to create mind maps, which are an efficient way to take notes from lectures or books. Brother Barry Buzan, who co-wrote *The Mind Map Book*, suggested the technique could also be used to capture notes from one's own creative ideas. Many sources, including the note books of Leonardo da Vinci, Albert Einstein, Pablo Picasso, Paul Klee and Winston Churchill have been found to contain notes or drawings that are similar to, or follow, a sub-set of the Mind Mapping rules.

"As a popular psychology author, Buzan has written on subjects relating to the brain, genius quotient (GQ), spiritual intelligence, memory, creativity and speed reading. He is President of the Brain Foundation, the founder of the Brain Trust Charity, the World Memory Championships and the World Championships of the Brain. He is also a co-founder of the Mind Sports Olympiad and London's Mind Body Spirit Festival. Buzan and his followers claim that his techniques can dramatically improve study performance and results."

For the original Cone of Learning research, see Edgar Dale, *Audio-visual methods in teaching* - New York: Dryden (1946, 1954, 1969).

The research suggesting that almost half of post-secondary students identify study skills as their greatest weakness is based on a 1995 survey conducted at Mohawk College in Hamilton, Ontario which asked over 4000 students to list their primary concerns as college students.

05 • BRAIN GROWTH

For many years, Bill Gates wrote a widely published syndicated column through the New York Times Syndication.

Concerning how much of our brains we really use, consider the research report, *Dormancy of the Human Brain*, by T.D.A. Lingo, Director of the Dormant Brain Research & Development Laboratory: "The human brain is only 10% functional, at best. The first to outline this theory, later proved a fact by others, was Australian Neurology Nobel Laureate Sir John Eccles (Lecture: University of Colorado, University Memorial Center Boulder, July 31, 1974.) 'The brain', he said, 'indicates its powers are endless.'

"In England, John Lorber did autopsies on hydrocephalics. This illness causes all but the 1/6th inch layer of brain tissue to be dissolved by acidic spinal fluid. He tested the IQs of patients before and during the disease. His findings showed that IQ remained constant up to death. Although over 90% of brain tissue was destroyed by the disease, it had no impact on what we consider to be normal intelligence.

"Russian neurosurgeon Alexandre Luria proved that the 1/3 bulk of frontal lobes are mostly dormant. He did this by performing ablation experiments on persons. He gave physiological and psychological tests before, cut out parts and whole frontal lobes, then re-tested after. His conclusion: removal of part or all of frontal lobes causes no major change in brain function (but some change in mood alteration). The frontal lobes are mostly dormant, asleep. (Luria, A.R. *Frontal Lobes and the Regulation of Behavior*. In: K.H. Pribram and A.R. Luria, Editors, *Psychophysiology of the Frontal Lobes*. New York, and London, Academic Press, 1973)

"Finally, the human brain contains 10 billion neurons, mostly in the outer layer of brain cortex. The function of these currently dominant cells is fairly clear, but the brain also contains 120 billion glial cells. Aside from some secondary nurturing of neurons, the primary function of the glia is not clear. What big bang miracle awaits mankind within these mysteries?

"Today, most would agree without argument that the potential of the human brain is infinite. Thus, to state that a person uses 10%, 5%, or even 1% of their potential brain capacity (infinity) is overly generous.

"The point is this: There is no dispute among honestly rational experts about the latent potential of the human think box. There is only friendly dispute about how much and what still awaits us, patiently to be self-discovered between each set of ears.

"Hence, the wisdom of intuitive folksay was correct: 'The human brain is only 10% functional.' John Eccles thinks that number is too high: 'How can you calculate a percentage of infinity?'"

For more from the two authors quoted with respect to the memory capacity of the human brain, see Richard Restak, *The Brain* - New York : Bantam Books, 1984 and Peter Russell (who worked with Tony Buzan in the 70s), *The Brain Book* - Dutton, New York, 1979.

'Building A Better Brain' by Daniel Golden, appeared as the cover story of the July 1994 issue of *Life* magazine. (Daniel Golden writes for *The Wall Street Journal*, where he has covered education since 1999. Previously, he was a reporter at the *Boston Globe*. The recipient of numerous journalistic honours and awards, including the Pulitzer Prize and the George Polk Award, he holds a B.A. from Harvard College.)

The Nun Study is directed by Dr. David Snowdon, a Professor of Neurology at the University of Kentucky's College of Medicine. He provides the answers to a number of questions below:

What is the Nun Study?

"The Nun Study is a longitudinal study of aging and Alzheimer's disease. It began in 1986 as a pilot study on aging and disability using data collected from the older School Sisters of Notre Dame living in Mankato, Minnesota. In 1990, the Nun Study was expanded to include older Notre Dames living in the midwestern, eastern, and southern regions of the United States. The goal of the Nun Study is to determine the causes and prevention of Alzheimer's disease, other brain diseases, and the mental and physical disability associated with old age."

How is the study funded?

"The Nun Study is funded by the National Institute on Aging (one of the institutes within the National Institutes on Health). More than $2 million in federal tax dollars have been invested so far in this study. In addition, private foundations including the Robert J. Kleberg, Jr. and Helen C. Kleberg Foundation in San Antonio, Texas, have given significant financial support to this endeavor."

When did the study begin?

"The University of Minnesota began a pilot study in 1986 using data collected from School Sisters of Notre Dame living in Mankato, Minnesota. When Dr. Snowdon joined the College of Medicine faculty at the University of Kentucky in 1990, the study was expanded to include older Notre Dames throughout the United States.

"The Nun Study is housed within the Sanders-Brown Center on Aging at the University of Kentucky Chandler Medical Center. The Center on Aging is internationally recognized for its research on the neuropathology of Alzheimer's disease."

For more information about dendrites and their growth, see the following website: *en.wikipedia.org/wiki/Dendrite.*

06 • BALANCING YOUR BRAIN

From Dr. Gordon Shaw, *Neurological Research* - University Of California, Irvine (1999): "In a study released (in 1998), second graders from a low- income school in Los Angeles were given eight months of piano keyboard training, as well as time playing with newly designed software. The result? These students, taking the Stanford 9 Math Test, went from scoring in the 30th to the 65th percentile.

"Dr. Shaw also explained that elementary school students at the 95th Street School in Los Angeles who took piano lessons boosted their math performance. In fact, the same researchers who conducted the 95th Street study have also found that the neural firing patterns at the most basic level of brain activity seem to resemble the patterns in music."

Willard R. Daggett, Ed.D., is President of the International Center for Leadership in Education. He has assisted a number of states and hundreds of school districts with their school improvement initiatives, many in response to No Child Left Behind and its yearly progress provisions.

Dr. Daggett has also collaborated with education ministries in several countries and with the Council of Chief State School Officers, the Bill & Melinda Gates Foundation, the National Governors Association, the U.S. Chamber of Commerce, and many other national organizations. (For more information, see *www.daggett.com/drdaggett.html.*)

07 • THE PERFECT BRAIN ENVIRONMENT

Just do a 'balanced brain' web search, and the list of references you'll get will keep you plenty busy for quite some time!

08 • BRAIN POWER

Be very careful with the list of 20 words that you learned in the second test. The fact is that every time you think about it — write it down, say it out loud, share it with others — the 'memory trace' will grow stronger and stronger. And, even when you think you've forgotten it, all it will take is a memory jogger of some kind to bring it back.

Case in point: Recently, after parking my car at the far end of a parking lot, I was walking towards a shopping mall. In the distance, I noticed a man who seemed to recognize me and started waving.

He then cupped his hands at his mouth and began reciting (shouting, actually) the list of 20 words. By the time he was finished, we were face to face. I didn't recognize him, but he told me he'd once attended one of my presentations. A year and a half prior to that day.

He'd been walking around with that meaningless list of words stuck in his brain for all that time, and all it took was seeing me, the Human Memory Jogger, to bring it all rushing back!

So, as I said, please be careful, OK?

09 • MOTIVATION

If you're interested in checking out more of Yoda's thoughts, try this website: *www.quotemountain.com/quotes/yoda_quotes/*.

Many websites have tips about remembering names. One of them is *www.cnn.com/2005/US/Careers/07/22/names/*.

10 • PRACTICE

For a number of insights about the relevance of rehearsal techniques, check out what Anne Pycha has to say in an article called *Why Practice Makes Perfect* at the following website: *www.brainconnection.com*.

11 • ASSOCIATION

Harry Lorayne was one of the first individuals to popularly write about using memory techniques to improve performance. With Jerry Lucas, he co-authored *The Memory Book: The Classic Guide to Improving Your Memory at Work, at School, and at Play* - New York: Ballantine Books (1986).

12 • MEANING

From *www.eduscapes.com*: "According to Jerome Bruner, meaningfulness is essential in learning. Dr. Bruner has had a profound effect on education – and upon those researchers and students he has worked with. His books include *The Process of Education*, *Toward a Theory of Instruction*, *The Relevance of Education*, and *The Culture of Education*."

13 • VISUALIZATION

Shakti Gawain's *Creative Visualization: Use the Power of Your Imagination to Create What You Want in Your Life* - New York: Bantam (1997) is considered a classic.

14 • CHUNKING

Patrick Lynch and Sarah Horton's *Web Style Guide* - Yale University, Yale University Press (2001) discusses the importance of chunking when designing websites, yet another useful modern application of George A. Miller's work from many years ago.

15 • EMOTION

From Wikipedia: "Emotionally arousing events are more likely to be recalled later than more neutral events, and the amygdala plays an important role in this enhancement as demonstrated by MRI studies showing that amygdala activation during encoding predicts later memory for emotional stimuli. (Canli, T., Zhao, Z., Brewer, J., Gabrieli, J.D.E., and Cahill, L. 2000)

"Activation in the human amygdala associates event-related arousal with later memory for individual emotional experience. The Journal of Neuroscience, 20, RC99 (1-5), as well as by a number of other studies (Hamann, S. – 2001). Cognitive and neural mechanisms of emotional memory. Trends in Cognitive Sciences, 5 (394-400); LaBar, K.S., & Cabeza, R. (2006). Cognitive neuroscience of emotional memory. Nature Reviews Neuroscience, 7, (54-64)."

16 • BRAIN GLUE

Joyce Wycoff is a co-founder of the Innovation Network, an organization focused on helping organizations develop a core competency of innovation. She's the author of *Mindmapping: Your Personal Guide to Exploring Creativity and Problem-Solving* - New York: Berkley Trade (1991), as well as several books on innovation and creativity.

17 • BRAIN TRICKS

Here's a website with a good list of mnemonics to help us remember facts, lists, etc.: *www.fun-with-words.com/mnemonics.html*.

18 • A GOOD IDEA

A web search for SQ4R will provide plenty of examples of this effective reading strategy. The University of Central Florida's Instructional Technology Resource Center gives a nice visual take of the technique (along with some interesting variations) at *www.itrc.ucf.edu/forpd/strategies/stratSQ4R.html*.

19 • A GREAT IDEA

More information and examples of mindmapping can be found in Peter Russell's *The Brain Book* (see Chapter 5 note) and in a number of books written by Tony Buzan that focus specifically on mindmapping techniques, including *The Mind Map Book: How to Use Radiant Thinking to Maximize Your Brain's Untapped Potential* by Tony & Barry Buzan: Plume; Reprint edition (March 1, 1996).

20 • BRAINS AT SCHOOL

York University's Counselling and Development Centre illustrates strategies like the Cornell Notetaking System and mindmapping: *www.yorku.ca/cdc/lsp/notesonline/note1.htm.*

21 • BRAINS AT WORK

From Wikipedia: "Alvin Toffler (born October 3, 1928) is an American writer and futurist, known for his works discussing the digital revolution, the communications revolution, the corporate revolution and technological singularity. A former associate editor of Fortune magazine, his early work focused on technology and its impact (through effects like information overload). Then he moved to examining the reaction of and changes in society."

Another great Toffler quote that has relevance to the ideas discussed in this book: "You've got to think about big things while you're doing small things, so that all the small things go in the right direction."

The University of Minnesota Duluth has the original Malcolm Forbes article, 'How To Write A Business Letter': *http://www.d.umn.edu/cla/faculty/troufs/comp3160/businessletter.html.*

ACKNOWLEDGMENTS

First of all, I have to thank my parents, Russell & Doreen, for bringing me into the world and for giving me what seems to be a pretty good brain to work with.

As well, I'm grateful to my in-laws, Ron & Barbara Wakeford, for sharing many excellent yarns with me and, in the process, helping me understand many of the the ins and outs of good storytelling.

My very favourite next-generation brains are my children: Dan, Luke and Jane. They've taught me plenty, in their own unique ways, about what brains can do in the 21st century. I'm happy to say that they appear to be figuring out how they like using their brains and, I think, are doing quite nicely so far. Touch wood.

My good friend, Steve Evans, was my early sounding board. He was in the audience at my initial public presentation and was the first to read my original manuscript, which he tactfully called "a real page-turner". I've often followed his wise counsel, and I'm grateful for his input. His brain must still be aching from listening to me talk about writing this book for all those years, so I'm happy — for him *and* for me — that it's finally done.

I'm indebted to Martin & Farah Perelmuter and everyone else at Speakers' Spotlight for giving me so many opportunities to offer 'brain training' to diverse organizations. I value their trust and am flattered by the confidence they continue to show in me.

I'd be remiss if I neglected to mention my trusty office assistant, a Jack Russell Terrier named Murphy who reminds me every single day that, if you always try really, *really* hard, then maybe — just maybe — you'll eventually end up getting what you want.

And, of course, I owe so much to my wife, Elizabeth. Her intelligence, her integrity, her sense of humour and her kindness are remarkable, and I'll be forever thankful that she's chosen to share her life with me.

I'm especially amazed, I have to say, that she's been able to teach me a significant lesson that has, quite frankly, taken me far too long to understand, learn and appreciate: that two brains really *are* better than one. (So long as they're the right two brains, of course.)

Revised in August 2011

Printed on 20# bond, certified chlorine-free, bleach-free, alkaline, 100% post-consumer recycled paper.

Cover by Samantha Murray, a graphic designer and webmaster extraordinaire who's been doing her best, for a number of years, to make Brian Thwaits look good.

Author's photograph by Jake Sheppard, an associate member of the family and official photographer of Brainspeaker Inc.

Brian Thwaits has taught and trained in both the public and private sectors for over 25 years. He began his academic career by winning a national student award at Lakehead University and concluded it by receiving the President's Award for Excellence from Mohawk College for his work both at the institution and in the community.

Brian is one of Canada's most accomplished and respected professional speakers, delivering presentations to the Department of Education in Hong Kong, the Learning Brain Expo in San Diego, Microsoft Canada in Toronto, the Athena Foundation in Chicago, the Canadian Police College in Ottawa, and Washington Mutual Bank in Anaheim — to name just a few organizations from an extensive international client list that is rapidly expanding as his reputation and success continue to grow.

His sessions cleverly combine the latest information from the disciplines of brain research, learning theory and the communication field to suggest innovative and practical approaches to issues we face in the workplace, in the classroom, and in our personal lives.

Please visit **www.brainspeaker.com** for more information about Brian Thwaits and his brain-training presentations.

ABOUT THE TYPEFACE

The typeface used in this book was designed by John Baskerville (1706-1775), who has been called "the greatest printer England ever produced".

A towering figure in the history of English typography, he broke one tradition and started another. Before Baskerville, the standard English type of the early 18th century was Caslon, a tradition which stretched back to Aldus Manutius of the 15th century. John Baskerville improved existing types, ink and presses and produced a clearer and blacker type than any of his contemporaries.

Unfortunately, his type was severely criticized due to the thinness of the strokes. Critics maintained that his type "hurt the eye" and would be "responsible for blinding the nation". It was a commercial failure and wasn't revived until the early 20th century.